THE FACE OF OUR PAST

edited by
Kathleen Thompson
& Hilary Mac Austin

with an Introduction by
Darlene Clark Hine

Indiana University Press
Bloomington & Indianapolis

The Face of Our Past

Images of

Black

Women

from

Colonial

America

to the

Present

This book is a publication of

Indiana University Press

601 North Morton Street

Bloomington, IN 47404-3797 USA

http://www.indiana.edu/~iupress

Telephone orders   800-842-6796

Fax orders   812-855-7931

Orders by e-mail   iuporder@indiana.edu

The paper used in this publication meets the minimum requirements of American National Standard for Information Sciences—Permanence of Paper for Printed Library Materials, ANSI Z39.48-1984.

Manufactured in the United States of America

Library of Congress Cataloging-in-Publication Data

The face of our past : images of Black women from colonial America to the present / edited by Kathleen Thompson and Hilary Mac Austin ; with an introduction by Darlene Clark Hine.

       p.   cm.

Includes bibliographical references.

ISBN 0-253-33635-X (alk. paper)

1. Afro-American women—History—Pictorial works.

2. Afro-American women—History. 3. Afro-American women—History—Sources. I. Thompson, Kathleen.

II. Austin, Hilary.

E185.86.F33   1999

920.72'08996073—dc21   99-24832

1 2 3 4 5 04 03 02 01 00 99

TITLE PAGES: These two tobacco tenant farm wives and their children lived in Wake County, North Carolina, in 1939. *Dorothea Lange. Farm Security Administration. Odum Photo Study, Southern Historical Collection, The Library of the University of North Carolina, Chapel Hill, negative #P-3167(B)-281.*

BACKGROUND PHOTO: Billie Holiday was perhaps the greatest jazz singer ever recorded. This photograph was taken about 1950 as a publicity shot for Columbia Records. *Photographs and Prints Division, Schomburg Center for Research in Black Culture, The New York Public Library, Astor Lenox and Tilden Foundations.*

Contents

Acknowledgments vii

Introduction by Darlene Clark Hine ix

FAMILY LIFE   1

WORK   29

HAIR   75

RESISTANCE   83

CLASS   127

EDUCATION   139

RELIGION AND COMMUNITY   161

PLAY   189

INNER LIFE   223

Archives and Collections 243

Image Sources 246

Text Sources 248

Illustration Credits 250

Index to Photographs and Quotations 257

Acknowledgments

THIS BOOK WOULD NOT HAVE BEEN possible without the generosity, advice, and patience of many people at archives and museums throughout the country. These people went beyond the call of duty to assist us.

We were lucky enough to be able to browse through a variety of photographic collections and archives. Invariably, we were treated with great generosity. At the Southern Historical Collection, John White and Richard Schraeder were extraordinary helpful. We are enormously grateful to David Haberstich at the Archives Center of the Smithsonian Institution. We would also like to thank Nicole Wells at the New-York Historical Society, Leslie Roland of the Freedman's Papers Project at the University of Maryland, College Park, and Rosemary Plakas and the reference librarians at the Prints and Photographs Division of the Library of Congress. Theresa Roan of the Valentine Museum and Charles Glover of the Black History Museum, both in Richmond, were very generous with time and information. Thanks should also go to Greg Kimball and Barbara Batson of the Library of Virginia for their leads on sources and their general interest in the project. Sister Virginie Fish of the Oblate Sisters of Providence provided a fascinating tour, a wonderful lunch, and inspiring conversation. Donna Wells of the Moorland-Spingarn Research Center was perpetually helpful and unstinting with her time, as was Jim Huffman of the Schomburg Center for Research in Black Culture.

In many cases, we were not able to travel to archives ourselves, and archivists kindly sent us images from their collections as well as leads to other sources. Among the many people who deserve special mention are Marianne Carden and Cathy Grosfils at the Colonial Williamsburg Foundation, Angela Bates-Tompkins of the Nicodemus Historical Society, Terry Hutchins of the Museum of the Confederacy, Erika Piola of the Library Company of Philadelphia, Mary Jean Blasdale of the New Bedford Whaling Museum/Old Dartmouth Historical Society, Carol Barber of the Wyoming State Archives, Alan Barnett of the Utah Historical Society, and Bonnie Morgan at the Montana Historical Society.

Other people who have been particularly generous and understanding include Ann Henry, John Magill of the Historic New Orleans Collection, John Lovett at the Western History Collection of the University of Oklahoma Library, Sherry Wilding White at the New Hampshire Historical Society, Will Harmon at the Division of Special Collections of the University of Oregon, and Mark Wright at the Smithsonian's Center for African American History and Culture. Jackie Burns of the J. Paul Getty Museum saved us on several occasions, and we cannot thank her enough for her knowledge and efficiency. Deborah Willis at the Smithsonian's Center for African American History and Culture deserves special mention here. She not only created the best reference works on the subject of black photographers, which were hugely helpful to us, but she has also shown us great kindness and support.

Kathy Clayton and Karen Creviston of the Amanda Park Branch of the Timberland Library system greatly facilitated the text research. Thanks are also due to the Northwestern University Library and the Chicago Public Library, particularly Cynthia Fife-Townsel, Michael Flug, and Andrea Telli. In the miscellaneously helpful category, we would like to give credit to the folks at the Pittsburgh Photographic Library, Betty at the Penn Center, Steven Niven and Jane Daley Witten at the Southern Historical Collection, the Lesbian Herstory Archives, Paul Carnehan at the Vermont Historical Society, and Chantalle Verna.

Thanks must also be given to the people who gave us access to and/or permission to reproduce images from their private collections: David Phillips, Currie Ballard, William Loren Katz, John and Linda Ravage, and Constance and Walter Dean Myers. Thanks to Winifred Haun, Lydia Ann Douglas, and Salimah Ali, who let us into their homes and allowed us to look through their pictures. A special thanks goes to Mr. Robert H. McNeill, a great photographer, a wonderful storyteller, and a true gentleman. We were very lucky that a few individuals granted us the honor of allowing us to use their family photographs. We thank them, their families, and the GoOnGirl Book Club, whose cooperation helped us find them. Beth Thomas not only showed us her private family photographs, she also gave us her insight and her time.

Nancy and Red Austin were receptionists, researchers, and cheerleaders. Without them this book would never have been completed. Michael Nowak was the constant throughout the project: supportive, opinionated, insightful, and a talented photographer in his own right. At Indiana University Press, John Gallman's faith in this project was unswerving, and Joe Phillips made the monetary aspects much easier and saner.

Thanks also to Paulette Carter and Eunice Hundseth for their invaluable eyes and memories, and to Melinda Hamilton, Karen Falk, Linda Werbish, Kristen Austin, Margaret Kale, and Jenny Bass, as well as Jennifer and Sargon at Quicker Printers. The following people know why they are being thanked: Craig Austin, Sara Thompson and Karen Konecky, Jim Schulz, and Jan Gleiter and Paul Thompson.

Finally, Darlene Clark Hine and Ralph Carlson truly made this book happen. To express fully our feelings about these two people and the help they have given us would undermine our credibility as rational and objective beings.

Introduction

CREATING AND DISSEMINATING a visual history is perhaps more important with Black women than with any other single segment of the American population. We know all too well what this society *believes* Black women look like. The stereotypes abound, from the Mammy to the maid, from the tragic mulatto to the dark temptress. America's perceptions of Black women are framed by a host of derogatory images and assumptions that proliferated during and in the aftermath of slavery and, with some permutations, exist even today. We have witnessed the distortion of the image of Black women in movies and on television. We have seen Black women's faces and bodies shamed and exploited. What we have not seen nearly enough is the simple truth of our complex and multidimensional lives. This book will eradicate, or at least dislodge, the many negative and dehumanizing stereotypes and caricatures of Black women that inhabit our consciousness and permeate the larger society.

Nannie Helen Burroughs was founder of the National Training School for Women (NTSW). She is pictured here (*left*) with an unidentified friend. On the back of the original photo is written "Douglas Improvement Company, Louisville, KY" and the title "A Happy Pair."

As Black history emerged as a respected and legitimate area of study, too little attention was devoted to exploring the contours and substance of the historical experiences of Black women. For the most part, Black women remained outside history. They were neither its primary subject nor its objects. When a Black women did make her appearance in the history books, she often seemed important only in conjunction with a man, an organization, or an institution.

Happily, this state of Black history has slowly but irrevocably changed. This is good news. We have traveled along two parallel paths, Black history and women's history, to bring Black women onto center stage. Working as hard as we could at the intersections of race and gender to create still another story, we have made considerable progress in our efforts to identify Black women and to answer the inevitable questions about who they are, what they think and feel and know, what they have contributed. One important question, however, demands more attention: What do Black women look like? What do we look like at work or with our families? What faces do we choose to present to the world, and what faces has the world forced us to assume? We can look in vain to most pictorial histories of America, and even of African America, for historical images of Black women. With noteworthy exceptions, even most scholarly studies in Black women's history contain few, if any, photographs.

There are many reasons for this void. Authors and publishers often consider the inclusion of illustrations to be a luxury they cannot afford, an unnecessary expense of little intrinsic value to the process of constructing history. To be sure, part of the difficulty is locating suitable representative images. This volume facilitates that process by making accessible fascinating and evocative photographs that future scholars and others may use to augment their works. Presented here is a veritable symphony of documentary images illuminating the vast array of features and frames found among both historical and contemporary Black women.

The International Sweethearts of Rhythm broke attendance records at such theaters as Chicago's Regal, Detroit's Paradise, and Washington, D.C.'s Howard, and they competed successfully in band polls that were otherwise exclusively male. Founded in 1939 as a fundraising group for Piney Woods Country Life School, they went out on their own in 1941 and began accepting a few white performers in 1943. This photograph shows a small part of the all-girl orchestra.

It is as difficult and as necessary to reclaim the images of Black women as it is to reclaim their story. In researching the facts of Black women's lives, we do have recourse to diverse public and private records, journals, letters, diaries, narratives and autobiographies, and other sources of the written word. These sources are somewhat limited because the majority of poor Black women were limited in their access to education and to the means of publication. Even more circumscribed was their access to the means of image creation, whether it was painting, engraving, or photography. Ironically, then, virtually all of the images of Black women that are extant from colonial America until well into the twentieth century were created by white men, white women, or Black men. (A notable early exception was, as historian Nell Painter tells us, Sojourner Truth, who exercised a great deal of control over her image.) The construction of a true picture of African American women, regardless of their class and geographical location, requires not only searching and digging to find individual images, but working with and around the biases of those who recorded them.

Of the images that have heretofore been presented in print, by far the majority of them have been of Black women whose activities have made them famous. The most popular book of contemporary photographs of Black women is *I Dream a World,* by Brian Lanker, and its portraits of women of distinction are as inspiring as they are beautiful. These women deserve, of course, the honor done them. But there is a need to go beyond the exceptional, to focus on the ordinary Black woman living her life, loving her family, working to survive, fighting for her people, and expressing her individuality.

This volume is an outgrowth of *A Shining Thread of Hope: The History of Black Women in America,* published in 1998 by Broadway Books. The photographic researcher on that book, Hilary Mac Austin, unearthed hundreds of images for me and my coauthor, Kathleen Thompson, to choose from. We were forced by the constraints of the project to limit ourselves to the sixty-seven that appeared in the pictorial inserts in that narrative history. *Black Women in America: An Historical Encyclopedia,* which I coedited with Elsa Barkley Brown and Rosalyn Terborg-Penn, and which was published in 1993 by Carlson Publishing (reprinted in paperback by Indiana University Press in 1995), also contained hundreds of photographs, but it was clear that, visually, even this was just a beginning. The response of readers to the images in these two publications revealed a strong desire for a more comprehensive, fresh, and truthful view of Black women. The present book emphasizes the lives, rather than just the accomplishments, of Black women. Each section spotlights a particular aspect of life, such as family life, work, community, or resistance to oppression.

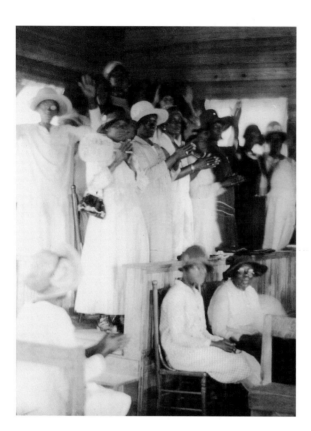

Photographer Doris Ulmann took this picture inside a country church on the Lang Syne plantation, South Carolina, sometime between 1929 and 1931 for *Roll, Jordan, Roll* by Julia Peterkin.

The Black family has long been viewed as the strongest institutional weapon of survival in African American culture and society. The flexibility of the Black family during slavery allowed it to accommodate many individuals other than blood relatives, providing crucial support to those who were robbed of actual kin. The extended family in freedom evolved largely because Black women provided the nurture and the care while men assumed, within the prescribed limits of a racist society, the roles of provider and protector, whether in slavery or in freedom. Black women bore the responsibility for maintaining kinship ties and for transmitting generationally the cultural values essential to heightened self-esteem and social activism. While enslaved women were often forced into socially constructed gender roles, there was something closer to equality in a slave family than in a traditional white, middle-class home. In the twentieth century, there was certainly more respect for alternatives to the patriarchal, two-parent nuclear family. Participation in cultural activities such as music-making, storytelling, and informal religious ceremonies was also much greater among Black women across the centuries than among white women. Some of this freedom came from the African heritage, the circumstances of slave life, and functional adaptation and resistance to white oppression in freedom. Whatever its sources, it was a very positive value.

In virtually every Black community in the country, Black women and men set up families, schools, churches, and health-care institutions. Given the barriers of racial discrimination, the virulence of white terrorist attacks, the reality of poverty, and formal political powerlessness, Black women in the age of Jim Crow discrimination had to create and sustain this separate infrastructure of support institutions. For them the twin engines of racial uplift and progress have always been institution building wedded to an oppositional consciousness and a culture of struggle.

The church served as the initial organizational base for Black women's benevolent, social welfare work. In innumerable church clubs, such as Daughters of Ham, the Eastern Star, and the Sisters of Zion, Black women performed invaluable service. To be sure, with rare exceptions, Black women did not preach in the pulpit, but they ministered to the sick, impoverished, and bereaved. When economic depression, bankruptcy, and disease struck the Black communities, the church women were there. They provided for the widows and the orphans. They taught Sunday school, did missionary work, and participated in endless fundraising drives. Most people would agree that the church rests most securely on the backs of Black women, whose work has enabled it to survive.

To generations of African Americans, education held the key to freedom and opportunity, and for Black women it possessed an even more potent value. Education offered a possible escape from sexual harassment, rape, and even domestic abuse. Black parents desired to educate all their children, and during the first couple of generations after slavery, more men than women pursued and earned baccalaureate degrees. When confronted with a choice, however, as to which child to educate in the face of dwindling resources, parents often chose their daughters. They knew from experience the degradation and sexual exploitation that domestic service work meant for Black women. Black parents reasoned that men were able to secure a more diverse range of jobs than women, and thus were not in as critical need of the family's and community's protection.

Throughout the late nineteenth and most of the twentieth century, education represented a community investment, and it was clearly understood that the educated children would return to assist in the uplift of the entire community. Early on, innumerable Black women became teachers in one-room schools. And because more was always expected of them, they also held classes in their homes and wrote books. Through it all, Black women have remained abiding champions of education as a means of personal autonomy and public empowerment.

Top: Black photographer Addison Scurlock took this photograph of his wife's cousin in 1907.

Bottom: Sisters Senora and Mary Brown had their portraits taken at the Tupper Studios in Greenwood, Mississippi, sometime during the 1920s.

A woman identified as "Po'" Mary, with an unidentified boy, posed for photographer Richard Samuel Roberts sometime in the 1920s. "Po'" Mary is said to have run a string of "boardinghouses" in Columbia, South Carolina. She charged 25 cents an hour for a room.

For white women, participation in public political life was long circumscribed. Black women, on the other hand, were not only allowed but expected to participate in the struggle for freedom. They have done so from the abolitionist era to the civil rights movement, and continue into the present to be forceful political advocates for justice for their people. Political action was on the agenda of every literary society and women's social club from the eighteenth century on. Freedom was a topic of conversation whenever Black women and men got together, whether it was over a laundry basket or at a dinner party. Still, there were some limits to women's participation in the various freedom movements. Even in the civil rights era they were often behind-the-scenes leaders, responsible for mobilizing communities. They were expected to work within "women's sphere" of fundraising and providing nurturing support. Sometimes they did. More often, they actually did most of the local level organizing essential to the success of political struggles that stretched from abolition to civil rights to Black Power.

But the lives of Black women were more than an endless struggle. In this book, we see dozens of images of women at play, laughing with each other, with their children, and with the men they love. We see friends at a table talking and little girls leaping for a ball on a school playground. In our lives, joy is a treasure, the more to be cherished, perhaps, because it is so hard won.

Yet the question remains, What is different about Black women? What makes them worthy of separate and distinct study? All women, in all times and places, have been concerned about family, education, community, and religion. Black women are no exception. Yet Black women *are* different, and the source of their difference is best reflected through an examination of their inner lives. How can we really come to know and understand their interior consciousness and fully appreciate their culture of struggle and resistance? The best means is to record and listen to their own personal voices. Here, among the images, are the words of Black women, completing the picture, so to speak.

It is apparent from the images and voices in this book that Black women are a diverse group. At the same time, we have certain important characteristics in common. The most readily apparent, even to the untutored observer, is our reliance on ourselves and each other. To say this is not to elevate us to the status of superwomen, but merely to observe a centuries-long process of adaptation to the American realities of sexual, racial, and class oppression. We have had two choices, either to become self-reliant and continually resist or to lay down our burdens and die. If most of us had chosen the latter course, there certainly would be little interest in or need to tell our story. Black women have struggled and survived. But, sadly, today larger numbers of Black women are dying; some are even taking their own lives. Why? Perhaps because the war against racial and sexual oppression and class exploitation hasn't been won. An examination of the lives and experiences of Black women through our history, individually and collectively, tells us to what extent the promises of democracy, justice, and equality remain unfulfilled. We need a better understanding of what our next step should be in trying to make those promises come true for all of us.

At no time in our history have we been in greater need of the wisdom, courage, and determination of our Black foremothers. Many Black communities today exist in a state of chaos, crisis, and conflict. There is no progress without survival, and our survival is currently precarious. However, at the risk of sounding sanguine, I believe there is power in history. To tap the hidden reservoirs of power, we must listen to the voices and look into the lives of the women who have brought us this far. In order to ensure that a new American history includes us all, it is imperative that we look at the face of our past.

Darlene Clark Hine
John A. Hannah Professor of History
Michigan State University

Relaxing while waiting to collect their pay, these migrant workers were photographed in the Homestead vicinity in February 1939.

THE FACE OF OUR PAST

IN MODERN AMERICAN MYTHOLOGY, a family is a group composed of a father, mother, and their children. The more enlightened recognize aunts, uncles, grandparents, and cousins as an integral part of the family unit. For African Americans, however, family is a much more flexible concept, and Black women have had to stretch to meet its requirements. The terrible exigencies of the institution of slavery tore husbands from their wives, children from their parents, and sisters from their brothers, but those who were enslaved held to the idea of family with a fierce intensity. It provided practical and emotional support in a world where survival demanded both.

Families in the enslaved community could and often did fit the nuclear mold. A surprising number of monogamous marriages with present husbands and fathers did exist. On the other hand, a stable, long-term family could also be made up of a mother and her children, a man and his brothers, an aunt and a nephew, or even a group of unrelated but emotionally committed fictive kin. The African heritage, with its emphasis on extended families and fictive kin, probably laid a foundation for this adaptable family unit and certainly helped enslaved people to work with the personal resources they had.

After emancipation, former slaves worked to reunite their families, sometimes spending decades trying to locate a lost child or a sister sold away in adolescence. There are personal advertisements from newspapers of the 1890s asking for information about family members separated by slavery. In the wake of the war that ended slavery, the Black family worked toward the mainstream ideal, but was again compelled by necessity to adapt. Free Black people of the eighteenth and nineteenth centuries frequently formed nontraditional families. Among those who reached some level of affluence, families were more conventional, it is true, but there was always a willingness to expand to meet the demands of the community. However, instead of viewing the flexibility of the family as a positive and enormously healthy aspect of Black life, many both within and without the community saw it as a sign of pathology.

In the twentieth century, criticism of the Black family increased, as "benevolent" social observers argued that slavery had unfitted African Americans for a normal family life. Others contended that it was the welfare system that destroyed the Black family. Not until the past few decades have some observers begun to recognize the reality of the situation. African Americans are so committed to the idea of family that they have adapted, adjusted, stretched, adopted, and done whatever was necessary to maintain families in spite of the obstacles placed in their way. And the Black family, far from being an undesirable result of slavery and economic oppression, is one of the reasons that African Americans have been able to survive those trials.

My great-great-grandmother was 120 years old when she died. She had seven children, and five of her boys were in the Revolutionary War. She was from Virginia, and was half Indian. . . .

My great-grandmother, one of her daughters, named Susanna, was married to Peter Simons, and was one hundred years old when she died, from a stroke of paralysis in Savannah. She was the mother of twenty-four children, twenty-three being girls. She was one of the noted midwives of her day. In 1820 my grandmother was born, and named after her grandmother, Dolly, and in 1833 she married Fortune Lambert Reed. Two children blessed their union, James and Hagar Ann. James died at the age of twelve years.

My mother was born in 1834. She married Raymond Baker in 1847. Nine children were born to them, three dying in infancy. I was the first born.

—Susie Baker King Taylor, *Reminiscences of My Life in Camp with the 33rd U.S. Colored Troops, Late 1st South Carolina Volunteers*

Eliza, Nellie, and Margaret Coplan were the daughters of a prosperous black businessman in Boston. They were painted in 1854 by W. M. Prior.

The first thing I recollect is living in a slave cabin back of Mars's big house, along with forty or fifty other slaves. All my childhood life, I can never remember seeing my pa or ma going to work or coming in from work in the daylight, as they went to the fields before day and worked til after dark. It was work, work, work, all the time. My ma worked in the fields up to the day I was born. I was born twixt the fields and the cabins. Ma was taken to the house on a horse.

—Jennie Webb, Federal Writers Project interview

Top right: From the *Anti-Slavery Almanac of 1840,* this illustration helped educate Northerners on the conditions of slavery.

Below: A family of field workers is shown in this 1842 collage by artist William Henry Brown. Brown was visiting a plantation near Vicksburg, Mississippi, when he created this portrait of an attractive family carrying the results of a week's work, and themselves, with pride.

About the middle of the evening, up rode my young master on his horse and up drove two strange white men in a buggy. They hitch their horses and come in the house, which scared me. Then, one of the strangers said, "Get your clothes, Mary. We has bought you from Mr. Shorter." I commenced crying and begging Mr. Shorter not to let them take me away. But he said, "Yes, Mary, I has sold you, and you must go with them." Then, those strange mens, whose names I ain't never knowed, took me and put me in the buggy and drove off with me, me hollering at the top of my voice and calling my ma.

—Mary Ferguson, Federal Writers Project interview

Left: Family life during the slave period was lived under the threat of sale. In this 1890 *Century Magazine* portrayal of an earlier period, a free man prepares to bid on the woman he is engaged to marry.

Below: This 1852 illustration for *Uncle Tom's Cabin,* based on a drawing by famed illustrator George Cruikshank, shows the separation of families during slavery.

Although most runaways had to leave their loved ones behind, a few families were able to escape slavery together via the Underground Railroad.

All over the country after the Civil War, families treasured these formal, posed photographs of "the Civil War soldier and his wife."

My mother came for us at the end of the year 1865, and demanded that her children be given up to her. This, mistress refused to do, and threatened to set the dogs on my mother if she did not at once leave the place. My mother went away, remained with some of the neighbors until supper time. Then she got a boy to tell [my sister] Caroline to come down to the fence. When she came, my mother told her to go back and get Henry and myself as quick as she could. Then my mother took Henry in her arms, and my sister carried me on her back. We climbed fences and crossed fields, and after several hours came to a little hut which my mother had secured on a plantation.

—Annie Burton, *Memories of Childhood's Slavery Days*

This 1872 engraving captures a universal moment, as a mother tells her son to "Go to sleep or Santa won't come." The artist, Sol Eytinge, was one of several artists whose work appeared in *Harper's Weekly* who seemed to have a desire to understand Black life and portray it truthfully. There were far more, however, whose work ridiculed, condescended to, and shamed Black Americans.

This strikingly sympathetic view of Black family life appeared in *Harper's Weekly* in 1888. The engraving is based on a painting by Thomas Hovenden.

This newlywed couple lived on the Rosemary plantation in Alabama around the turn of the century. The wife or daughter of the owner of the estate created several scrapbooks of photographs she had taken of the plantation's Black workers. Although the captions reflect the biases of the society in which the photographer lived, her photographs reveal the humanity of her subjects. This image from the album "Rosemary, a Plantation Home" was entitled simply *The Newlyweds.*

Below: Love and dignity mark this image of an unidentified woman and her husband, Brutus, in 1906 on Palawana Island, S.C. Leigh Richmond Miner photographed the couple for the book *Face of an Island,* by Edith M. Dabbs.

LeAnna Samuels (*seated*) and her three daughters, Harriet, Margaret, and Mary (*left to right*), posed in front of their home in Nicodemus, Kansas, one of the first Black towns founded by the Exodusters in the late 19th century.

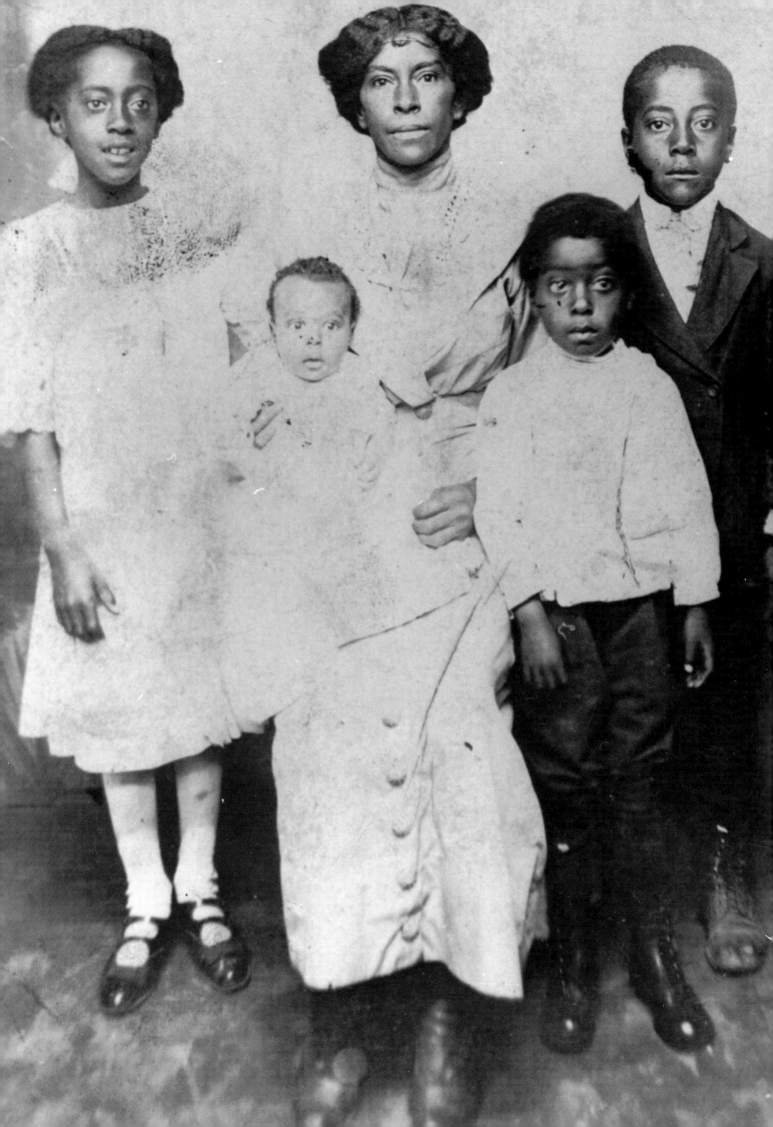

Left: A middle-class mother and her children posed for their portrait in Utah at the turn of the century.

Right: A grandmother posed with her granddaughters in this 1920s portrait by Richard Samuel Roberts.

Below: The family of Moses and Sarah Jane Turner Gaskin Johnson posed for this photograph in Cheyenne, Wyoming, in March 1921, after the funeral service for Pearl Gaskin Edwards. The family matriarch is at the center of the picture, holding the youngest grandchild, Lloyd. Among those missing from the picture is Ethel Gaskin, who was in college in Nebraska at the time.

Isabella Heywood, a graduate of the Penn School in South Carolina, is shown here with her baby Mary Isabel on the steps of Hampton House on the school's campus in about 1910.

Men and women are not made on trains and streetcars. If in our homes there is implanted in the hearts of our children, of our young men and our young women, the thought that they are what they are, not by environment, but of themselves, this effort to teach a lesson of inferiority will be futile.

—Nannie Helen Burroughs

This photograph, taken about 1913, is appropriately entitled *Big Sister.*

In another photograph from the Rosemary plantation scrapbooks, a woman combs the hair of a young girl, possibly her daughter, in a ritual known and treasured by most Black women. This image was captioned *The Givers* by the photographer.

This young couple was part of the Gullah community on Lang Syne Island, photographed by
Doris Ulmann in 1929–30 for *Roll, Jordan, Roll,* by Julia Peterkin.

A family of migrant workers posed in the late 1930s. *Collier*

Top right: This little girl was part of a tenant farm family who lived on the Milestone plantation in the Delta area of Mississippi in November 1939. She was standing in the "kitchen" of the family's home. *Marion Post Wolcott.*

Bottom right: This family was photographed outside a store and barber-shop in Union Point, Georgia, on a Saturday afternoon, possibly waiting for the husband and father to get his hair cut. *Jack Delano.*

Below: The children in this photograph taken in Georgia in 1941 were eating white clay.

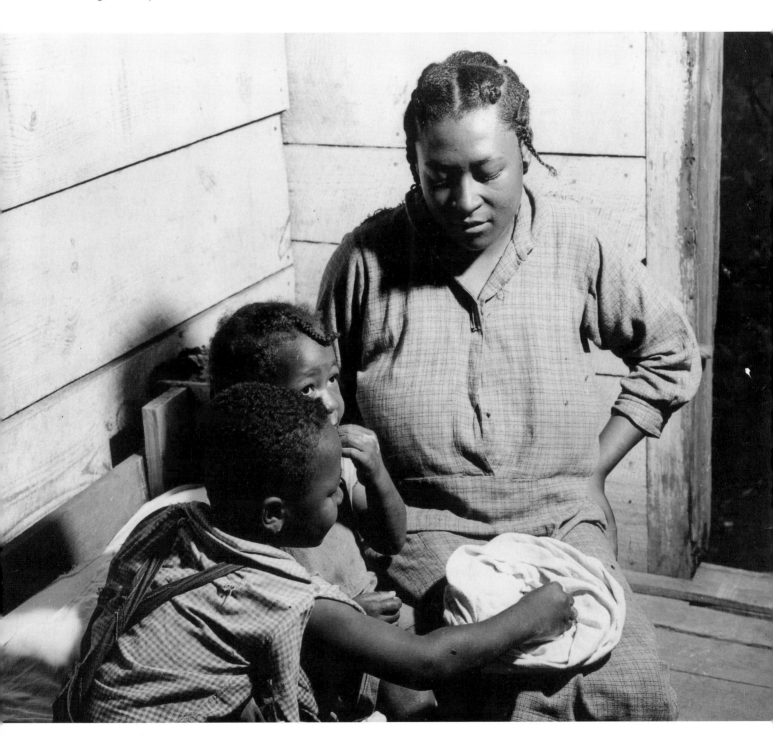

In Texas Parish, Louisiana, in the late 1930s, this woman went to school for the first time at the age of 65. Her adopted son, who was 16 and in the second year of high school, was not eligible for the WPA literacy classes and didn't need them, but he accompanied his mother to school every night to help her with her lessons.

Mrs. Ella Patterson and her great-grandson pose in front of a treasured family photograph in this 1942 portrait. They were among the first residents of the new Ida B. Wells housing project in Chicago, Illinois. *Jack Delano.*

When we prepare for a journey, when we enter on a new undertaking, when we decide on where to go to school, if we want to shop, to move, to go to the theatre, to eat (outside of our own homes) we think quite consciously, "If we can pull it through without some white person interfering."

—Jessie Fauset, *The World Tomorrow* (New York), March 1922

Photographer Dorothea Lange captured this woman eyeing beans and bananas in a grocery store somewhere in North Carolina in 1939.

This woman held up snapshots of her three soldier sons in June 1943 in
Placquemines Parish, Louisiana. *John Vachon.*

On Memorial Day 1943, two women decorated a soldier's grave in a Black section of Arlington National Cemetery. In 1941, Roosevelt had issued an Executive Order forbidding racial and religious discrimination in defense work. *Esther Bubley.*

One of the little poems of Paul Lawrence Dunbar that I learned way back, says, "A crust of bread and a corner to sleep in." Well, I didn't want a crust of bread. I wanted that soft, yeasty inside. And I didn't want a corner to sleep in. I wanted a house to sleep in. And then the poem says, "A minute to laugh and an hour to weep in." Well, I didn't want that. I wanted an hour to laugh in and the minute to weep in. Next it says, "A pint of joy to a peck of trouble." You know I didn't want that. And I didn't want this other part that says, "Never a laugh but the mourns come double, and that's life." We propose to do something better.

—Cassie Swarm, Black Women in the Middle West Project

Family activities in the Black community could include resistance work. Rosa Parks (*left*) and her mother, Leona McCauley (*right*), attended the Highlander Folk School together to learn strategies for school desegregation from Septima Poinsette Clark in December 1946.

Right: Anna Laura Lee poses next to her father, J. R. E. Lee, Jr., on Anna's wedding day, December 22, 1953, in Tallahassee, Florida.

Right: A mother smiles down at her child in this photograph from the famed Scurlock family of Black photographers.

Below: A mother held her crying baby as her furniture was put on the sidewalk during an eviction in the 1950s. *Austin Hansen.*

In this still from the film *Nappy,* Asha plays a game while her mother, Cassandra, fixes her hair. *Michelle Marion.*

Ife and Raven at the beach in New London, Connecticut, in 1992. *Lydia Ann Douglas.*

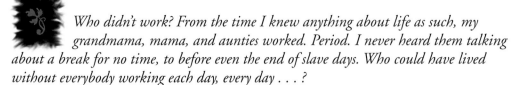

Who didn't work? From the time I knew anything about life as such, my grandmama, mama, and aunties worked. Period. I never heard them talking about a break for no time, to before even the end of slave days. Who could have lived without everybody working each day, every day . . . ?

—"Darethia Handy," born 1897 in East Texas, quoted in
Living In, Living Out, by Elizabeth Clark-Lewis

ONE OF THE MAJOR demands of the modern feminist movement has been the right for women to work outside the home. That demand may have been the single most difficult one for Black women to line up behind, since so many of them had been struggling so long for the right *not* to work but to stay at home with their families. The history of African American women has been a history of work. They were brought to this country to work. During slavery, work devoured their time and invaded the most private parts of their lives. The conditions of their working lives involved beatings, humiliation, sexual abuse, and every form of deprivation.

After emancipation, Black families focused great energy and attention on protecting women from the horrors they had faced as enslaved workers. Keeping mothers and their daughters out of white men's fields and white women's kitchens was a priority second only to food and shelter for the family. However, it was a priority the family was seldom able to maintain, as Beverly Guy-Sheftall points out in *Daughters of Sorrow: Attitudes toward Black Women, 1880–1920.* "In 1910, twenty-six out of every hundred Black married women worked; in 1920, thirty-three out of every hundred worked, whereas in the same decade only six married white women out of every hundred were gainfully employed. Over one-third of all African American women continued to work as field laborers or wage earners even after they reached sixty-five."

The vast majority of Black women who worked were employed as field laborers or domestic workers. Factory work was rarely open to Black women, and white-collar work was all but impossible to obtain. A privileged few were able to acquire the education necessary to become professionals such as doctors, lawyers, and teachers. Others, such as Madame C. J. Walker, America's first self-made woman millionaire, rose from field work or domestic service to build their own businesses. In spite of their circumstances, Black women managed to carry out their working lives with dignity and, surprisingly often, some satisfaction. They also managed to care for and rear their children, support their churches, and better their communities at the same time.

In recent years, work and its implications have changed for all women in American society, and for none more than Black women. While the majority of Black women workers still work as domestics or in other poorly paid jobs, there was a 125 percent increase in the number of Black professional women between 1982 and 1992. In 1994, a dozen Black women sat on the boards of directors of at least three Fortune 500 companies. And in 1995, there was one Black woman, Oprah Winfrey, among the four hundred richest people in America. Moreover, Black women own or control more than one-third of the 400,000 Black-owned businesses in the United States. Today, Black women are transforming work and the role it plays in their lives.

This 18th-century engraving depicts a West African village thought to be somewhere in Senegal. The image of the two women pounding grain is mirrored in photographs of southern American Black women dating as late as the 1930s.

This watercolor on paper by Benjamin Henry Latrobe, ironically entitled *Overseer Doing His Duty*, was painted from a scene near Fredericksburg, Virginia, and is dated March 3, 1798.

Showing how slavery improves the condition of the female sex.

The last whipping Old Mis' give me she tied me to a tree and—oh, my Lord—she whipped me that day. That was the worst whipping I ever got in my life. I cried and bucked and hollered, until I couldn't. I give up for dead, and she wouldn't stop. . . . I stop crying and said to her, "Old Mis', if I were you and you were me, I wouldn't beat you this way." That struck Old Mis's heart, and she let me go, and she did not have the heart to beat me anymore.

—Sarah Douglas, Federal Writers Project interview

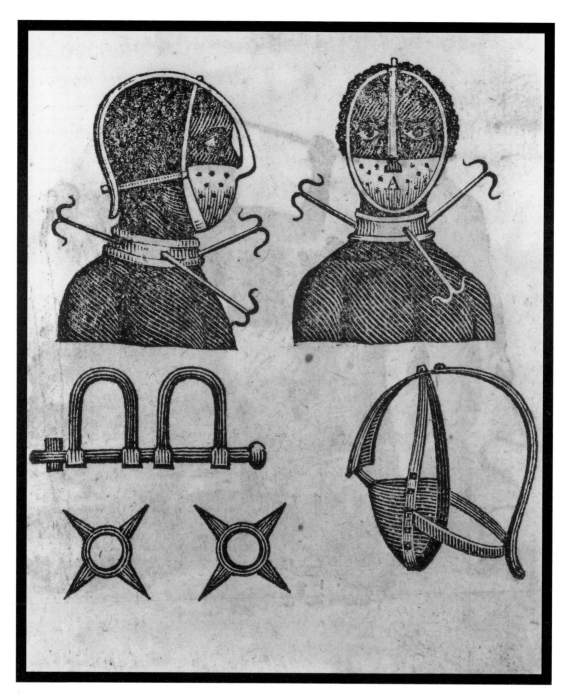

This illustration of the collars, shackles, and masks that disobedient slaves were forced to wear was used in Thomas Branagan's 1807 book *The Penitential Tyrant.* It has become one of the most common images used to illustrate the cruelty of American slavery.

Left: From the *Anti-Slavery Almanac of 1840,* this engraving and others like it were used in many different abolitionist and anti-slavery publications, including the *Narrative of the Life and Adventure of Henry Bibb.*

This woman selling chicken legs and rolls at the Richmond, Virginia, train station may have been either a free woman or a slave. She was sketched on October 6, 1860, by Sir Henry Wentworth Acland and was included in his *Sketches in North America: Sarnia, United States and Home.*

I was a lady's maid. I'd wait on my mistress, and I'd knit socks for all the folks. When they would sleep, it was our duty—us maids—to fan them with fans made out of turkey feathers—feather fans. Part of it was to keep them cool. Then, they didn't have screens, like we have today, so part of it was to keep the flies off. I remember how we couldn't stomp our feet to keep the flies from biting, for fear of waking them up.

—Mattie Mooreman, Federal Writers Project interview

Most upper-class white children in the South were reared by Black women, such as the one depicted in this ca. 1850 daguerreotype by an unknown photographer. The occasion of a young child's portrait was usually the only time a slave would be photographed.

I gets to thinking now how Wash Hodges sold off Maw's children. He'd sell them and have the folks come for them when my maw was in the fields. When she'd come back, she' raise a ruckus. Then, many's the time I seed her plop right down to a-setting and cry about it. . . . She said, "O, Lawd, let me see the end of it before I die. . . ."

—Lulu Wilson, Federal Writers Project interview

Free Black women held a large variety of occupations and were among America's earliest female entrepreneurs. This oil painting, done in 1845 by artist William Sidney Mount, is entitled *Eel Spearing at Setauket*.

Elleanor Eldridge, born in 1784, owned a successful painting and wallpapering business in Providence, Rhode Island. This image was the frontispiece of *The Memoirs of Elleanor Eldridge*, published in 1832. She is shown holding a wallpaper brush.

Facing page: Born a slave, Elizabeth Keckley bought her freedom and rose to become Mary Todd Lincoln's dress designer.

Outside of the Fort were many skulls lying about; I have often moved them one side out of the path. The comrades and I would have wondered a bit as to which side of the war the men fought on, some said they were the skulls of our boys; some said they were the enemies; but as there was no definite way to know, it was never decided which could lay claim to them. They were a gruesome sight, those fleshless heads and grinning jaws, but by this time I had become used to worse things and did not feel as I would have earlier in my camp life.

—Susie Baker King Taylor, Union Army nurse, from *Reminiscences of My Life in Camp with the 33rd U.S. Colored Troops, Late 1st South Carolina Volunteers*

Above: Black women were involved at all levels of Army life during the Civil War, from Harriet Tubman, who planned raids for the Union Army, to Mrs. Fairfax, who is depicted here. The fact that Mrs. Fairfax was identified in this 1863 photograph is in itself unusual. That she is referred to by her surname, and with the possibly fond identification of "chief cook & bottle washer," indicates a certain level of respect.

Left: Susie Baker King Taylor was born a slave. She became a laundress and then a nurse during the Civil War. Her memoirs are among the most moving and informative documents of the period.

I'se been working for owner three years, and made with my children two bales cotton last year, two more this year. I'se a flat-footed person and don't know much, but I knows those two bales cotton fetch enough money, and I don't see what I'se got for them. When I take my little bit of money and go to the store, buy cloth, find it so dear, dear Jesus!—the money all gone and leave, children naked. Some people go out yonder and plant cotton for theyself. Now they get big piles of money for they cotton, and leave we people way back. That's what I'se looking on . . .

—Old Grace, worker on Sea Islands plantation,
demanding better terms from planter

Top left: During the Civil War, liberated slaves (contrabands) worked on plantations on the Sea Islands that had been confiscated from their Confederate owners. This photograph was taken in 1862 by Henry P. Moore when his Union regiment, the 3rd New Hampshire, was in control of the Sea Islands. It shows a woman drying cotton on a wharf on Edisto Island in South Carolina.

In another 1862 photograph by Henry P. Moore, contrabands plant sweet potatoes on an Edisto Island plantation.

Clara Barton and the Red Cross went to the Sea Islands to do relief work in the 1890s. As part of its program, the Red Cross provided seed potatoes. These women are cutting the potatoes for planting.

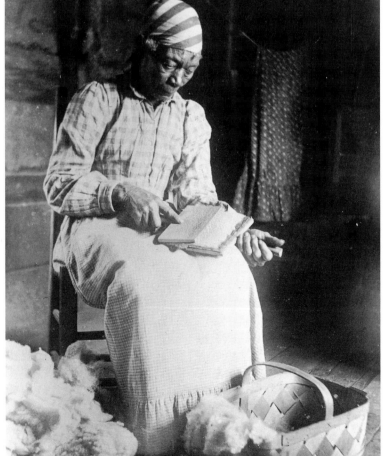

Above: While a small minority of Black women were able to become professionals, most continued to do domestic or field work, as in this ca. 1887 photograph by Rudolph Eichemeyer.

Left: "Aunt Ca'ine," a worker on the Rosemary plantation, was carding when this photograph was taken.

Preachers don't know nothing about hell. They ain't worked in a tobacco factory.

—Louise Harris

Virtually the only industrial work Black women could get was in tobacco factories. In this detail from a photograph by Huestis Cook, these women are shown stemming tobacco in the 1890s.

Below: The workers in a tobacco factory gathered outside for this picture in the 1890s.

This unidentified young woman was either a student or a faculty member at the National Training School for Women, which was founded in 1901 by the Women's Convention of the Black Baptist Church.

Carlotta Stewart-Lai moved from Brooklyn, New York, to Hawaii in 1898 and became a high school principal. Her family's affluence and her principal's salary allowed her to dress beautifully and to travel.

A family of musicians and entertainers homesteaded in the 1880s and 1890s near Westerville in Custer County, Nebraska.

Top right: "Stagecoach" Mary Fields is one of the most famous Black women of the Old West. She was Gary Cooper's childhood idol, and it is in part through his reminiscences of her that she was saved from historical obscurity.

Bottom right: Milly Ringold was a rancher and miner in Utica, Montana. She is shown here in front of her claim, the Weatherwax Mine.

This is the woman whom civilization has passed by. But it is from her loins, no less than from the earth itself, that the world's greatest cotton industry has sprung. A slave, and a breeder of slaves, hundreds of thousands of her kind have been crushed in its gigantic and merciless machinery. And as long as the tenant system continues, she must be sacrificed to its greed.

—Elaine Ellis, *The Crisis,* October 1938

Cutting sugar cane in the early 1920s, this woman looks strikingly similar to the Georgia field worker in the following photograph, taken in 1895. For poor rural workers in the South, not much changed in dress or technology from slavery times until well into the 20th century.

This Georgia field worker, photographed in Thomasville, Georgia, ca. 1895, has intricately wrapped her headcloth as protection against the sun and shortened her skirt with a cord tied around her hips, both traditional among African American women workers. *A.W. Moller.*

As part of the "Great Migration" north, this group waited with their worldly goods at the Union Railroad Depot in Jacksonville, Florida, in 1921.

Right: World War I led to more factory work for Black women. This photograph by F. P. Burke, taken on April 16, 1919, was originally entitled *Negro Women Weighing Wire Coils and Recording Weights, to Establish Wage Rates.*

Below: Many women who traveled north found that the only work available to them was domestic work. This image by an unknown photographer was taken in Washington, D.C., about 1910 to show the architecture of the concrete wall in the background.

Gentlemen: I read [Chicago] Defender every week and see so much good youre doing for the southern people & would like to know if you do the same for me as I am thinking of coming to Chicago about the first of June, and wants a position. I have very fine references if needed. I am a widow of 28. No children, not a relative living and I can do first class work as house maid and dining room or care for invalid ladies.

I am honest and neat and refined with a fairly good education. I would like a position where I could live on places, because it is very trying for a good girl to be out in a large city by self among strangers is why I would like a good home with good people. Trusting to hear from you.

—"A Widow of 28," from New Orleans

Left: This photograph, entitled *The Herbalist,* was probably taken in Louisiana or South Carolina between 1929 and 1931. It may have been created for use in the book *Roll, Jordan, Roll,* about Gullah life on Lang Syne plantation. *Doris Ulmann.*

Right: Dr. Justina Ford practiced medicine in Denver in the 1920s.

Eunice Hunton Carter, who in 1935 became the first Black woman district attorney in New York, was one of the "twenty against the underworld," as special prosecutor Thomas E. Dewey called his prosecution team.

During the Depression, economic problems became even worse for Black women, as for others. Some of the women waiting for domestic work in this 1939 photograph entitled *Jobline* may have been waitresses, factory workers, or even teachers before the Crash. *Harold Corsini.*

My cousin told me about up here. The other day I didn't have a cent in my pocket and I just had to find work in order to get back home and so I took the first thing that turned up. I went to work about 11 o'clock and I stayed until 5 o'clock—washing windows, scrubbing floors and washing out stinking baby things. I was surprised when she gave me lunch. You know, some of them don't even do that. When I got through, she gave me thirty-five cents. Said she took a quarter out for lunch. Figure it out for yourself. Ten cents an hour!

—Millie Jones, quoted by Ella Baker and Marvel Cooke, *The Crisis*, November 1935

Above: Aptly entitled *Carrying Laundry Home*, this photo was taken in Durham County, North Carolina, in 1939. *Marion Post Wolcott.*

Bottom left: Photographer Robert H. McNeill was commissioned by *Fortune* magazine to take a series of photographs of the Bronx slave market for an accompanying article. The article, entitled "The Servant Problem," was published in March 1938, without Mr. McNeill's pictures. Ultimately the photographs were published in *Flash* magazine as well as the Chicago *Defender*. The *Flash* caption for this image read: "Labor Wins. Housewife and 'slave' bargained 40 minutes for 5¢ an hour wage difference. A good bout!"

My people worked for over thirty years in North Carolina growing tobacco and crops. There was never a year they made a dime or a difference.

—"Ophilia Simpson," quoted by Elizabeth Clark-Lewis in *Living In, Living Out*

Above: This woman and her husband owned their own farm and were able to keep it throughout the Depression.

Top right: This woman plowed the ground in 1930 in much the same way her grandmother might have done a century before. *Doris Ulmann.*

Bottom right: A barefooted farm worker planted sweet potatoes in Person County, North Carolina, in 1939.

61

When I first went to the shipyard, I was a file clerk. And then they were training the women on the cranes . . . you had to climb all those catwalks. . . . I'm not going to say I wasn't afraid, I was. But I wasn't going to give [the men] the benefit of the doubt of knowing it. They had the wall cranes but they didn't pay as much money as the 20 tons, so that's what I wanted. You . . . had three months to qualify and . . . six months to make your first rating. So I kept going up until I got to be a first mate's crane operator on the 20 ton crane. That's the one that lays the keels for the submarines, the cradle, and the engines, torpedo tubes, anything like that. I worked on those 110 feet in the air. So I did that during wartime.

—Rosary B. Cooper, Black History of Seacoast New Hampshire, Oral History

"Rosie the riveter." These women, photographed in June 1943, were welders at the Landers, Frary and Clark Plant in New Britain, Connecticut. *Gordon Parks.*

Left: Surrounded by a sea of silk, this woman sewed parachutes for American paratroopers in an aircraft factory at an East Coast navy yard in May 1942. *Liberman.*

Right: After fighting for decades for the right to serve, Black nurses such as this one arriving in the European theater of operations were accepted into the military in World War II.

The 688th Central Postal Battalion was the first all-Black female unit to ship overseas.
The 800 women of the battalion served in England and handled mail for the entire European
theater of operations.

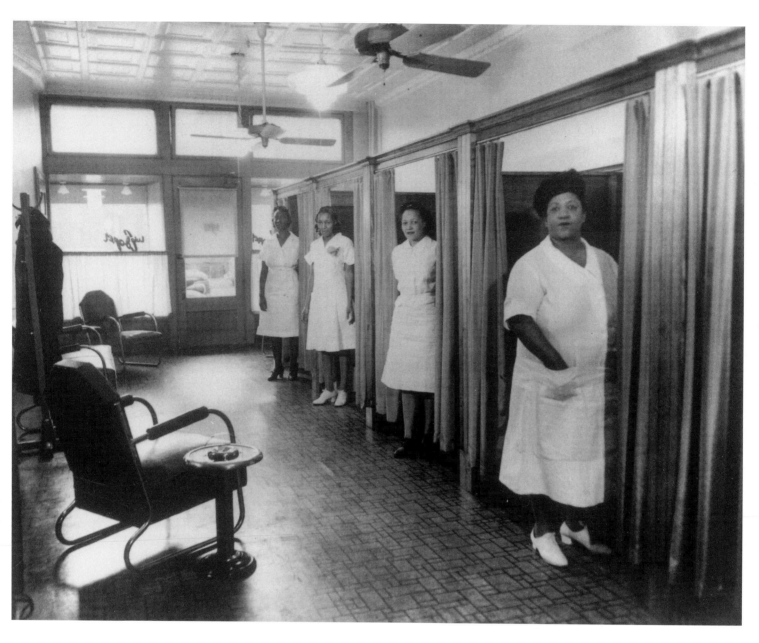

Beauty shops, such as the Lula B. Cooper French Beauty Salon in Washington, D.C. (1939), have long been an important form of entrepreneurship for Black women. *Robert H. McNeill.*

Marion's Place was a "juke joint" in the Glades area of south-central Florida.
This photograph was taken in February 1941. *Marion Post Wolcott.*

These women operated a luncheonette in the Shaw area of Washington,
D.C., in the late 1930s. *Robert H. McNeill.*

This 1962 photograph shows a woman in South Carolina being paid $3.00 for the bale of cotton she had just picked. *Bruce Davidson.*

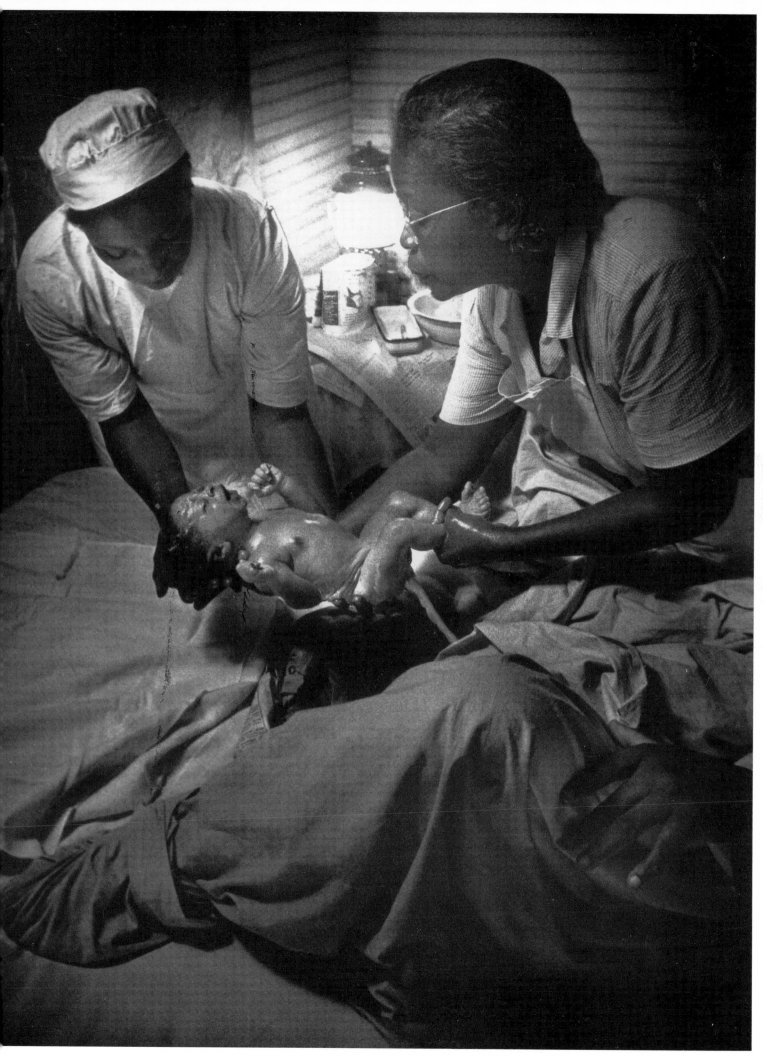

Taken as part of a photo essay by W. Eugene Smith, this 1951 image captures licensed nurse-midwife Maude Callen as she holds the child she has just delivered. At the time this photograph was taken, Callen was responsible for the health care of thousands of rural people.

Left: Cheryl Miller led the U.S. women's basketball team to a gold medal in the 1984 Olympics and has since gone on to a career in sports broadcasting.

Bishop Barbara Harris was the first female bishop in the history of the Episcopal Church. She is shown here blessing the congregation after her ordination on February 12, 1989.

Isabell Monk is one of America's most gifted theatrical actors. She is shown here playing Iphigeneia in Euripides' *Iphigeneia at Aulis. Michael Daniel.*

We have loved in a space where love was not meant to be. We have measured our lives in sacrifices for our children and our men, and when we could no longer ignore our own needs, we have stood in defense of ourselves. . . .

We have led revolutions—quiet and otherwise—and done it with style and grace. Even our hair is an expression of who we are: braids or locks, finger waves or weaves, perms or Afro puffs. We are finding ways to define ourselves, and in the process redefine America.

　　　　　　　　　　　—Marcia D. Davis, 1996

Marva Collins founded the Westside Preparatory School in Chicago as an alternative to a failing public school system.

Mable Whittington is a waitress at the Little Corner Diner in Chicago. *Michael Nowak.*

Lillian Roberts owns Natural Resources, an herb and gift store in Chicago. *Michael Nowak.*

Since 1988, Carole Simpson has anchored ABC's *World News Saturday. Brent Peterson.*

Mrs. Vera Harrison took time off every afternoon from her responsibilities operating a florist shop in downtown Richmond, Virginia, to sell flowers at a street stand. She was photographed on September 25, 1979, for the *Richmond Times-Dispatch. Tommy Price.*

Overleaf: In this still from the film *Nappy,* made in 1997,
Asha gets her hair washed. *Michelle Marion.*

Good hair—That's the expression. We all know it, begin to hear it when we are small children. When we are sitting between the legs of mothers and sisters getting our hair combed. Good hair is hair that is not kinky, hair that does not feel like balls of steel wool, hair that does not take hours to comb, hair that does not need tons of grease to untangle, hair that is long. Real good hair is straight hair, hair like white folks' hair. Yet no one says so. No one says Your hair is so nice, so beautiful because it is like white folks' hair. We pretend that the standards we measure our beauty by are our own invention—that it is questions of time and money that lead us to make distinctions between good hair and bad hair.

—bell hooks, *Bone Black: Memories of Girlhood*

I am alive because of the blood of proud people who never scraped or begged or apologized for what they were. They lived asking only one thing of this world, to be allowed to be. . . . And I learned through the blood of these people that Black isn't beautiful and it isn't ugly, Black is. It's not kinky hair and it's not straight hair—it just is.

—Gloria Naylor, *The Women of Brewster Place*

Showing a diversity of hairstyles worthy of a modern braiding salon, this engraving from the 1816 travels of J .B. Debret was originally captioned *Esclaves Nègres de Différentes Nations.*

Aida Overton Walker was not only one of the most beautiful women of her time, she was one of the most talented. Working with her husband, George Walker, in the Williams and Walker musicals, she became an international superstar.

This *carte-de-visite* photograph is of an unidentified woman in Helena, Montana, in the 1890s. Also unknown is the person who did her hair!

Right: Ethelyn Taylor Chisum was a dean at Booker T. Washington High School in Dallas for 32 years. Her modified Gibson Girl hairdo was fashionable but dignified enough for her position.

Lily Armstrong Shaw's 1898 wedding picture, taken in a Kansas studio, shows a hairstyle that was remarkably natural for the period.

Above: Broadcast journalist Norma Quarles.

Top left: Singer Joyce Bryant's silver hair was her trademark during the fifties, when she was a national phenomenon, the subject of Walter Winchell interviews and *Life* magazine layouts. The color was achieved with silver radiator paint. This photo was taken on May 28, 1953, by Carl Van Vechten.

Left: A 1940 photograph of a woman working in a tobacco factory shows a neat braided style.

Below: These two lovely young women are identified as "two daughters of Buck Grant, a preacher." The photograph was taken in June 1941. *Jack Delano.*

Congo Locks, a portrait of Melody in Seattle, Washington, 1997. *Lydia Ann Douglas.*

RESISTANCE IS A LARGE ISSUE in the lives of African American women. It encompasses everything from the slave revolts of the eighteenth century to the affirmation of African identity in the last years of the twentieth. Resistance includes the small ways in which enslaved women thwarted the demands of their owners and the massive social action of the 1950s and 1960s. It is a continuing theme in the history of Black women.

Overleaf: Justice. *Declan Haun.* © *Estate of Declan Haun.*

Women resisted slavery in all the ways that men did—revolts, running away, refusal to obey an owner's commands. But there were differences. Women ran away less often, for example, and seem to have resisted specific working conditions more often. They were frequently the preservers of African traditions in clothing, cooking, and medicine. They also resisted the concept of ownership in a powerful way by fighting to preserve their sexual integrity. Tens of thousands of enslaved women endured beatings, persecution, and even death in order to assert that the control of sexual access to their bodies belonged to them.

Women were involved in some of the earliest legal challenges to slavery, as well. In 1765, Jenny Slew sued for her freedom in a Massachusetts court and won. In 1780, Elizabeth Freeman, also known as Mum Bett, went to court maintaining that, since the Massachusetts state constitution declared all men free and equal, slavery was illegal. Illiterate herself, she found a lawyer to present her case and won.

Black women were the foundation of the abolitionist struggle, as organizers and fundraisers. Some also broke through the conventions of the day to become speakers and leaders in the movement. It was in the service of abolition that Maria W. Stewart became the first American woman of any race or color to speak publicly in front of a group of both men and women. Harriet Tubman and many other Black women risked their lives on the Underground Railroad, working to help thousands escape slavery.

During the Civil War, Black women recruited soldiers, traveled with the Union Army as cooks and nurses, and even served as spies. Mary Elizabeth Bowser, for example, feigned feeblemindedness while employed as a servant in Jefferson Davis's Confederate White House in order to garner intelligence to smuggle to Union officers. Another Black woman, a seamstress, helped in the smuggling effort by working coded messages into the dress patterns she carried with her.

Jim Crow brought out the fierce determination of Black women to preserve their community. They formed clubs to care for the young and the aged, founded schools and hospitals, and acted as virtually the sole source of social services for the Black community in America. Those clubs, along with the church organizations for which Black women were the lifeblood, served as training grounds in resistance. When the civil rights movement of the 1950s required organizational skills, Black women were there.

To this day, women are in the forefront of the Black resistance struggle as workers, mothers, artists, and activists. At the same time, they are leaders in organizations that support all women and groups that work to help all our children. The spirit of resistance remains very much alive in America's Black women.

There are two stories relating to this image from *A Portraiture of Domestic Slavery . . . by Jesse Torrey* (Philadelphia, 1817). The first is that she was an escaped slave and jumped to avoid recapture. The second is that she attempted suicide after her children were sold away from her. She broke her back and both her arms.

Although this engraving is from an 1890 *Century Magazine*, it fairly accurately reflects the transport of new slaves from the interior of West Africa to the coast, where they would be sold to European and American slave traders.

Many slaves came to America via the West Indies. This ca. 1850 engraving shows the "examination" of human beings for sale in the islands. © *Collection of the New-York Historical Society.*

This engraving from the *Anti-Slavery Record* of September 1835 illustrated the story of an enslaved woman in Marion County, Missouri. Upon learning that her two sons were to be sold away from her, she killed them and then herself.

This engraving illustrates an event reported in the *Anti-Slavery Record* of February 1836. A woman named Harriet was freed by her owner. It was promised that Harriet's children would be manumitted as well, but the owner's grandson kept them in slavery. As adults, they escaped and joined their mother. When the slave holder traced the eldest son, James, and sought to return him to slavery, Harriet begged him to remember his grandmother's wishes, saying, "I suckled you at the breast, and now you drag my children away from me to send them to slavery!"

This painting by an unknown artist, ca. 1810, is aptly and disturbingly entitled *Virginian Luxuries*. The sexual abuse and rape of enslaved women by their male owners is a subject that still brings fervent denials from some white Southerners even today. Yet, there is no doubt that such abuse was common.

About the worst thing that I ever seed . . . was a slave woman at Louisburg who had been sold off from her three-weeks-old baby, and was being marched to New Orleans. She had walked till she was give out, and she was weak enough to fall in the middle of the road. She was chained with twenty or thirty other slaves, and they stopped to rest in the shade of a big oak while the speculators et their dinner. The slaves ain't having no dinner. As I pass by, this woman begs me in God's name for a drink of water, and I gives it to her. I ain't never been so sorry for nobody.

It was in the month of August, and the sun was bearing down hot when the slaves and their drivers leave the shade. They walk for a piece, and this woman fall out. She dies there 'side of the road, and right there they buries her, cussing, they tells me, about losing money on her.

—Josephine Smith, Federal Writers Project interview

A famous photograph of an enslaved man's scarred back mirrors this *Harper's Weekly* engraving of a formerly enslaved woman (date unknown). Enslaved women were just as likely to be "disciplined" by flogging as men.

There was one of two things I had a right to, liberty, or death; if I could not have one, I would have the other; for no man should take me alive.

—Harriet Tubman

Above: At the young age of fifteen, Maria Weems escaped from slavery by dressing as a young man.

Left: When Harriet Tubman, also known as "Moses," reached the free state of Pennsylvania, she recalled, "I looked at my hands to see if I was the same person. There was such a glory over everything, the sun came like gold through the trees, and over the fields, and I felt like I was in heaven." She later made repeated trips into the South to bring back freedom seekers.

Sarah Parker Remond had a profound effect on British audiences during the more than forty-five antislavery speeches she gave in England between 1858 and 1861.

No writer can describe the slave's life; it cannot be told; the fullest description ever given to the world does but skim over the surface of this subject. You may infer something of the state of society in the Southern States when I tell you there are eight hundred thousand mulattoes, nine-tenths of whom are the children of white fathers, and these are constantly sold by their parents, for the slave follows the condition of the mother. . . . When I walk through the streets of Manchester and meet load after load of cotton, I think of those eighty thousand cotton plantations on which was grown the one hundred and twenty-five millions of dollars' worth of cotton which supply your market, and I remember that not one cent of that money ever reached the hands of the laborers. . . . Now I ask for your sympathy and your influence, and whoever asked English men and women in vain? Give us the power of your public opinion, it has great weight in America.

—Sarah Parker Remond, speaking in Manchester, England, in September 1859. She remained in England after the Civil War to enlist support for the Union.

A small minority of Black abolitionists supported the colonization movement and moved to Liberia. Mrs. Urias R. McGill was living there with her husband when this photograph was taken by Augustus Washington.

My beloved brethren, as Christ has died in vain for those who will not accept his offered mercy, so will it be vain for the advocates of freedom to spend their breath in our behalf, unless with united hearts and souls you make some mighty efforts to raise your sons and daughters from the horrible state of servitude and degradation in which they are placed. . . . Did the pilgrims, when they first landed on these shores, quietly compose themselves and say, "The Britons have all the money and all the power, and we must continue their servants forever"? . . . No, they first made powerful efforts to raise themselves, and then God raised up those illustrious patriots, WASHINGTON and LAFAYETTE, to assist and defend them. And, my brethren, have you made a powerful effort?

—Maria W. Stewart, lecture delivered at the Franklin Hall, 1832

Sojourner Truth, born Isabella Bomefree, began speaking against slavery and for women's rights in the 1840s.

Below: This symbol was widely used by the abolitionist movement. Am I not a woman?

'Am I not a Woman and a Sister?'

RESISTANCE ❦ 95

$ 50.00 Reward !!

Ran away from the Yard Corner of Jackson & Broad Streets, Augusta Ga. — on the evening of Tuesday 7th April 1863 a Woman "Dolly", whose likeness is here seen. —

She is thirty years of age, light Complexion — hesitates somewhat when spoken to, and is not a very healthy woman — but rather good looking, with a fine set of teeth. Never changed her Owner and has been a house Servant always. — It is thought she has been enticed off by some White Man, being herself a Stranger to this City, and belonging to a Charleston Family. —

For further particulars apply to Antoine Poullain Esq. Augusta Ga. —

Augusta Police Station

Louis Manigault Owner of Dolly

This reward poster was found as part of a plantation owner's journal. During the Civil War, thousands of slaves smelled freedom in the air and fled their masters. Strangely, Louis Manigault, Dolly's owner, felt she was "enticed off by some White Man."

When slaves headed for freedom during the Civil War, they generally fled to Union lines. The Union Army, after dithering for some time about what to do with these refugees, decided that they were "contrabands of war" and stopped returning them to their owners. Many contraband women served as cooks, laundresses, and nurses for the Union Army.

My husband Julius Leach was a member of Co. D. 5" U.S. C[olored] Cavalry and was killed at the Salt Works Va. about six months ago. . . . When my husband was Killed my master whipped me severely saying my husband had gone into the army to fight against white folks and he my master would let me know that I was foolish to let my husband go he would "take it out of my back," he would "Kill me by piecemeal" and he hoped "that the last one of the nigger soldiers would be Killed" He whipped me twice after that using similar expressions The last whipping he gave me he took me into the Kitchen tied my hands tore all my clothes off until I was entirely naked, bent me down, placed my head between his Knees, then whipped me most unmercifully until my back was lacerated all over, the blood oozing out in several places so that I could not wear my underclothes without their becoming saturated with blood. The marks are still visible on my back. On this and other occasions my master whipped me for no other cause than my husband having enlisted. When he had whipped me he said "never mind God dam you when I am done with you tomorrow you never will live no more." I knew he would carry out his threats so that night about 10 o'clock I took my babe and travelled to Arnolds Depot where I took the Cars to Lexington I have five children, I left them all with my master except the youngest and I want to get them but I dare not go near my master knowing he would whip me again.

—Affidavit of Patsy Leach, 25 March 1865, *The Black Military Experience*
Belair [*Md.*] Aug 25th 1864

This woman posed in front of an empty slave pen, owned by the firm of Price, Birch & Co., "Slave Dealers" in Alexandria, Virginia. The photograph may have been taken by William R. Pywell, in August 1862 or 1863.

Mr president It is my Desire to be free. to go see my people on the eastern shore. my mistress wont let me you will please let me know if we are free. and what can I do. I write to you for advice. please send me word this week. or as soon as possible and oblidge.

—Annie Davis, in a letter to President Abraham Lincoln

George Mears, shown here with his wife, was a Democratic state representative after Reconstruction.

Below: Black women were always involved in politics, even before they had the vote. This February 6, 1869 engraving from *Harper's Weekly* of the attendees at the National Colored Convention in Washington, D.C., shows that it was not just an "old boys' club."

I understand you to say, then, you saw four men killed under the circumstances stated, and that you know in addition of two others being killed, and that then you saw the dead body of this girl, Rachael? *Yes, sir; and my brother got killed Tuesday afternoon; who killed him I do not know.*

What was his name? *His name was Bob Taylor. He had been a member of the 59th Regiment, but was out of service. On Tuesday afternoon when they were firing and going from house to house, I told him to try to get away by the bayou just back of my house. He was older than I am. They robbed me that night of $300 of his money.*

This September 14, 1867 engraving from *Harper's Weekly* illustrates an event that took place in North Carolina during the violent days of Reconstruction. The author of the accompanying article wrote in part: "No single act of inhumanity has more clearly indicated the animosity yet existing in Southern hearts against the former slaves; or shown how unwise it would be to trust the government of these people in the hands of their former masters." *W. L. Sheppard.*

Entitled *Visit of the Ku Klux,* this February 24, 1872 engraving from *Harper's Weekly* depicts the early terrorist activities of the Ku Klux Klan. *Frank Bellew.*

Did they come to your house? *Yes; a crowd of men came in that night. I do not know who they were. They just broke the door open and asked me where was my husband; I replied he was gone; they said I was a liar; I said, "Please do not do anything to me; I am just here with two little children."*

Did they do anything to you? *They done a very bad act.*

Did they ravish you? *Yes, sir.*

How many of them? *There was but one that did it. Another man said, "Let that woman alone—that she was not in any situation to be doing that."*

What did they mean by saying you was not in a condition to be doing that? *I have been in the family way since Christmas.*

> —From a congressional investigation into one of several mass slaughters in 1866 of Black men who had served in the Union Army. It was determined that forty-six African Americans and two white radicals were killed, at least seventy-five more people wounded, and five Black women raped in this Memphis massacre.

Above: The ruins of Richmond, Virginia serve as backdrop for this photograph of formerly enslaved Americans leaving the city by boat on April 2, 1865.

When we got in sight of Nicodemus the men shouted, "There is Nicodemus." Being very sick I hailed this news with gladness. I looked with all the eyes I had. I said, "Where is Nicodemus? I don't see it." My husband pointed out various smokes coming out of the ground and said, "That is Nicodemus." The families lived in dugouts. The scenery to me was not at all inviting and I began to cry. . . .

Days, weeks, months, and years passed and I became reconciled to my home. We improved the farm and lived there nearly twenty years, making visits to Nicodemus to attend church, entertainments, and other celebrations.

—Williana Hickman, *Topeka Daily Capitol,* August 29, 1939

Above: This is a detail of a larger picture entitled *Refugees on Levee* and is dated April 17, 1897. In the three decades or so following the Civil War, thousands of former slaves left the South.

Below: Many former slaves headed west, participating in the great American dream of the new land and new life west of the Mississippi. This picture is entitled *Covered Wagon Days in Wyoming, Overland Trail,* ca. 1870s.

Henry B. Worth described the circumstances surrounding this picture in his book *Photographs of Old Dartmouth:* "For many years before its removal, the John Howland House was occupied by colored people. When the property was purchased by the Fall River Cotton Brokers, they ordered the tenant Mrs. Mann to vacate. She refused and they proceeded to demolish the house. They took out the windows and doors and had begun to tear down the chimney when she decided it was time to move. This picture represents the last of her household effects while she was waiting for a vehicle to transfer them to another part of the city." *Fred Palmer.*

The Libby, McNeil, Libby plant was photographed by the *Chicago Daily News* in 1904, two years before Upton Sinclair's *The Jungle* exposed horrifying occupational diseases and hazards in the Chicago stockyards.

In 1920, Christia Adair took some schoolchildren to meet the train when Republican Warren G. Harding was campaigning for the presidency. After seeing him shake hands only with the white children, she became a Democrat.

Below: This woman sat in the back of a Black Maria after race riots devastated parts of Tulsa, Oklahoma, in 1921.

She stands now at the gateway of this new era of civilization. . . . To be alive at such an epoch is a privilege, to be a woman then is sublime. . . . changes of such moment are in progress, such new and alluring vistas are opening out before us, such original and radical suggestions for adjustment of labor and capital, of government and the governed, of the family, the church and the state, that to be a possible factor . . . in such a movement is pregnant with hope and weighty with responsibility. To be a woman in such an age carries with it privilege and an opportunity never implied before.

—Anna Julia Cooper (1858–1964), *A Voice from the South by a Black Woman from the South* (1892)

Left: Because of the Southern strategy adopted by much of the white woman suffrage movement, Black women formed their own organizations to fight for the right to vote and then to exercise that right. The organization shown here had its headquarters in Georgia in the early part of this century.

Below: Maggie Lena Walker's Order of St. Luke was a powerful advocate of Black freedom and equality through economic self-reliance. This billboard reflects the evangelical nature of the message.

The Independent Order of Saint Luke

BENEFITS FOR ALL IN OUR MARCH TO SUCCESS

In 1920, the Montana State Federation of Colored Women's Clubs met for the first time.
This picture was taken to commemorate the event and was kept as a family treasure,
with handwritten identifications. The federation remained active until the 1970s.

→ Alice Brown

Cora Johnson

Mrs Riddly Clay

Bea Simms

→ Mrs Green (Becky's mother in law)

Floyd Walker

Mrs Irvin

→ Rose Glen

Aunt Ethel

Grandmother Fisher

Ella Banks

Emma Harrell

Frances McDuffie (Audrey Walker's mother)

Above: The Housewives' League of Detroit was founded in 1930 for the purpose of keeping Black money in the Black community and using economic power to obtain jobs for Black workers. By 1934, the league had 10,000 members.

Left: These families were evicted from their homes on the Dibble plantation near Parkin, Arkansas. Because they belonged to the Southern Tenant Farmers' Union, they were charged with, and convicted of, "conspiracy to retain their homes." Their eviction, therefore, though at the point of a gun, was quite legal. *John Vachon.*

The Sharecroppers Union, the Tenant League, and many of the newly organized unions owe their existence to the unselfish contributions of Negro women. . . . Organized labor owes women as a class more than a union book.

—Sabina Martinez, Organizer for the Amalgamated Clothing Workers
of America, *The Aframerican,* Summer and Fall 1941

The story behind this picture, taken in 1911, was horrifyingly common in the South in the early 20th century. The lynched man had been accused of raping a white woman. The man, naturally in fear for his life, ran to his mother's house, where the lynch mob caught up with him. Both mother and son were killed. During this period, such photographs of lynchings were turned into postcards.

If the Southern citizens lynch Negroes because "that is the only successful method of dealing with a certain class of crimes," then that class of crimes [rape] should be shown unmistakably by this record. . . . But the record makes no such disclosure. Instead, it shows that five women have been lynched, put to death with unspeakable savagery, during the past five years. They certainly were not under the ban of the outlawing crime. It shows that men, not a few, but hundreds, have been lynched for misdemeanors, while others have suffered death for no offense known to the law, the causes assigned being "mistaken identity," "insult," "bad reputation," "unpopularity," "violating contract," "running quarantine," "giving evidence," "frightening children by shooting at rabbits," etc. . . . Instead of being the sole cause of lynching, the crime upon which lynchers build their defense furnishes the least victims for the mob. In 1896 less than thirty-nine per cent of the Negroes lynched were charged with this crime; in 1897, less than eighteen per cent; in 1898, less than sixteen per cent; in 1899, less than fourteen per cent; and in 1900, less than fifteen per cent were so charged.

—Ida B. Wells-Barnett, *The Independent,* May 16, 1901

This Howard University student wears a symbolic noose at a 1934 demonstration protesting the omission of lynching from the agenda of a national conference on crime.

Signs such as this one in the window of the First Market Lunchroom
in Richmond, Virginia, were common throughout the South during
Jim Crow days.

We couldn't go to a restroom. We did buy gasoline at a lot of gas stations, but we couldn't go to a white restroom, so we would have to drive through the country and find a spot in the woods where the children could go. The same problem held true for cafes and lunchrooms. . . . We would stop at stores and buy food, milk, ice cream, and fruit, and then we would have a picnic lunch. We usually had to travel day and night, because we couldn't find desirable places to spend the night. We couldn't go to a white hotel, and there were very few colored hotels or schools that could accommodate a sizeable group. . . . Usually when we went to those track meets, it would take all day, all night, and sometimes the next day, and that's the way we did it.

—Jessie Abbott, Schlesinger Black Women Oral History Project

In 1954, in Baxley, Georgia, local landowners gathered in the white high school's gymnasium for a town meeting. Photographer David R. Phillips captured the scene. Chairs were provided for the white men on the gymnasium floor. Black men—and one lone woman—sat in the bleachers. © *David R. Phillips.*

Before Emmett Till's murder, I had known the fear of hunger, hell, and the Devil. But now there was a new fear known to me—the fear of being killed just because I was black.

—Anne Moody, Coming of Age in Mississippi

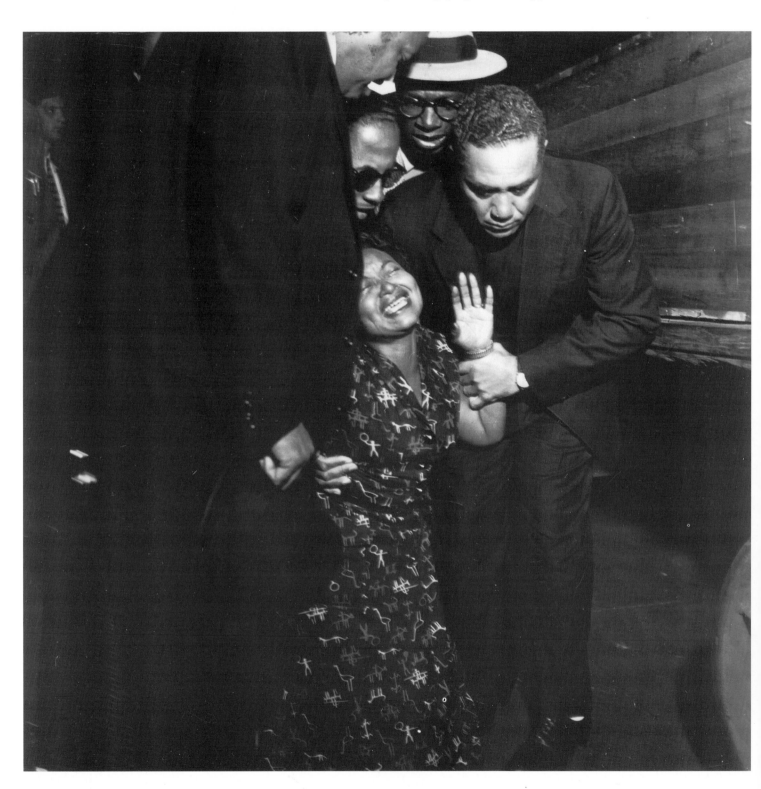

Mamie Bradley collapsed when she met the coffin of her son, Emmett Till, as it arrived in Chicago. The fifteen-year-old was killed while visiting relatives in Mississippi for the "crime" of whistling at a white woman. *William Lanier.*

Members of the "Little Rock Nine" attempted to speak with a National Guardsman during the integration battle of 1957. The students are Carlotta Walls, unidentified, Gloria Ray, and Ernest Green.

This woman was arrested during a demonstration in Birmingham, Alabama, in 1963. *Bruce Davidson.*

An early Black Panther march, possibly in Lourdes County, Alabama, in 1966. *Laurence Henry.*

Left: Daisy Bates, president of the Little Rock NAACP and organizer of the integration of Central High School, picketed three downtown department stores in Little Rock, Arkansas.

These women express joy and pride as they watch the Freedom March
from Selma to Montgomery in 1965. *James Karales.*

March on Washington, 1963. *Declan Haun. © Estate of Declan Haun.*

Above: A marcher following the Reverend Martin Luther King Jr. into the white suburb of Cicero, Illinois, expressed the militancy that developed in the late sixties. *Declan Haun.* © *Estate of Declan Haun.*

Right: Nancy Gooding stands in the tradition of social welfare activists that includes such greats as Eva Del Vakia Bowles, Lugenia Burns Hope, and Victoria Earle Matthews. *Philip A. Greene.*

We Americans have come to feel that it is our mission to make the world free. We believe that we are the good guys, everywhere—in Vietnam, in Latin America, wherever we go. We believe we are the good guys at home, too. When the Kerner Commission told America what black Americans had always known, that prejudice and hatred built the nation's slums, maintain them and profit by them, white America would not believe it. But it is true. Unless we start to fight and defeat the enemies of poverty and racism in our own country and make our talk of equality and opportunity ring true, we are exposed as hypocrites in the eyes of the world when we talk about making other people free.

—Shirley Chisholm, first speech in the U.S. House of Representatives, March 16, 1969

Shirley Chisholm talked with young supporters on March 25, 1972, after announcing her bid for the presidency at the Massachusetts presidential primary.

For me, feminism is not White. Feminism is something that Black women have attempted to define and have been eloquent about since the 1870s. What we need to do is to claim that movement and talk about the ways in which we have actually been more revolutionary and more progressive around gender issues than White women have. But as long as we give it up to them, then we won't be as much in touch with our history.

—Beverly Guy-Sheftall, feminist writer and editor, *Emerge,* March 1995

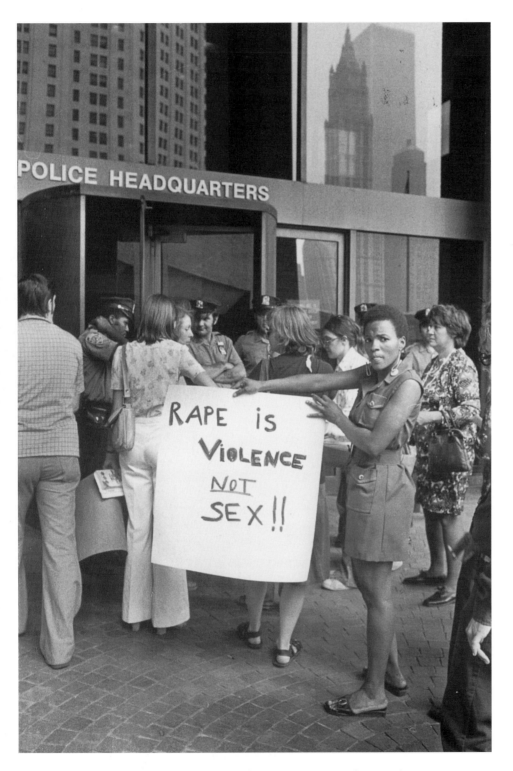

Above: Black women were among the first to file lawsuits under Title VII of the Civil Rights Act to define the crime of sexual harassment. When law professor Anita Hill reluctantly testified that she had been harassed by Supreme Court nominee Clarence Thomas, the face of government in America may have changed forever. *Rick Wilking.*

Right: This pro-choice demonstrator was photographed while participating in a candlelight rally at the state capitol in Austin, Texas, on the anniversary of *Roe v. Wade,* June 1989. *Alan Pogue.*

Demonstrators protest the handling of rape cases at New York City police headquarters, August 28, 1974. *Bettye Lane.*

"Without the Right to own and control her own body, no woman can be considered free"

Margaret Sanger

Security women at the Million Woman March.
Salimah Ali. © Salimah Ali, 1997.

Today, we put America on notice—we do not march for the sake of marching—we do not rally in the rain and the cold because we have nothing else to do. We are driven by our commitment to ourselves, our children and our families to live in a fair and just society that respects us and our role in this nation and in this world.

—Maxine Waters, speech at the Million Woman March, October 25, 1997

MY MOTHER WAS A single African-American woman raising seven kids with little income and even less opportunity. During my childhood, she became an abusive alcoholic.

Now stop right there, sugar. Up in your mind a tape is beginning to play that tells you, "Oh, yeah, I know what *that* means. She's Black and she was poor. *Swing low.* She's gonna be angry, and she—"

But that's someone else's movie. There's more to my life than that. Yes, we did have a hard time, and, yes, I have a lot of anger. But you have to work hard at getting me angry. Or you have to be a politician and not work at all. Just watch out when I start to move my neck.

There's more to my story than the poor, Black girl from the projects. I am also the first person in my family to attend, let alone graduate from, college, and I went from there to get a Ph.D. in sociology. . . . I spent a year as the host of my own nationally syndicated talk show, and I am a stand-up comic who's funny without ever talking about somebody else's mother or how I "do it."

Overleaf: This woman near Hinesville, Georgia, was living in an old army camp in April of 1941 after losing her sharecrop during the Depression. She told the photographer that she had no plans for the future.
Jack Delano.

Along the way, I've been a janitor, a bingo-caller, and I worked in a shelter for battered women. I've been a post office employee, a food-stamp bureaucrat, a teacher, and amicably divorced. I am also a single mother. There you go again with that moving picture of dirty children and a tired, sex-crazed woman in a food-stamp line. That movie was written by folks who don't know me or any other real people. They are the scriptwriters who use words like *jive* and *hip* and call women "Sweet Mammy." Please, who talks like that?

In actuality I've never had children of my own. I'm raising my sister's three children and we don't qualify for food stamps. But if we did, I wouldn't be embarrassed to use them.

There's a lot more to my experience than anything that tape in your head will tell you. I'm sure that there are folks who have done what I've done and who have been through what I've been through. But not all at once and not in one lifetime. Or maybe there have been and I'm the only one who's still running around loose.

—Bertice Berry, *Bertice: The World According to Me*

This early daguerreotype (1850–53) shows an unidentified free woman. It is possible that she was Elizabeth Denison Forth, who left $1,500 in her will for the construction of the Saint James Protestant Episcopal Chapel in Grosse Ile, Michigan.

The original caption of this December 31, 1908, mug shot reads as follows: "New Orleans Police Department. Bertha Farnsworth. Alias: Bertha Rawlings. Occupation: Washwoman. Criminal Occupation: Susp. Person. Nativity: Miss."

This painting on glass is by an unknown artist, possibly Charles Zechel, made at an unknown date. The clothing has been identified as 17th-century Dutch and accurately reflects how a Black woman might have looked in New York in the 1650s.

Right: Most photographs of enslaved women, unless they were posed with white children, were actually taken in the years following the Civil War. This detail is from a larger photograph of Drayton's plantation at Hilton Head taken in 1862, before Emancipation. *Henry P. Moore.*

Nancy Weston lived in Charleston, South Carolina, in the 1850s as a free woman.
However, in order to satisfy the laws of the state, she was a nominal slave, legally owned
by a white friend. She was the grandmother of writer Angelina Weld Grimké.

Anna Hyers and her sister Emma were operatic singers, child prodigies who grew up to found, in 1875, the first professional black repertory company. The company produced musical plays about the black experience in America. This publicity photograph was probably taken in the 1870s.

Left: Taken in 1907, this photograph shows a rice worker, identified as Adelaide, on St. Helena Island, South Carolina. She is wearing the traditional wrapped headcloth and hip cord. The baskets she carries are also probably based on traditional African methods and designs. *Leigh Richmond Miner.*

Right: Clara Keaton, who was born in 1798, was the first depositor at the National Savings and Trust Bank in Baltimore. This photograph, thought to date from the 1870s, was probably taken to commemorate the deposit.

Damange Tolliver Duesse was the first Black child on record born in the Wyoming Territory. Her family's affluence is apparent in her clothing and the accessories of the household that surround her in this picture, thought to have been taken in the 1890s. *Edgar D. Meyers.*

This Aultman Studio portrait, taken in the 1890s, shows a woman identified as Jenny Shears, who is wearing an atypical natural hairstyle. The fact that she was photographed in a nightgown suggests that she may have been a prostitute.

Above: Photographer Doris Ulmann captured this woman ironing between 1929 and 1930.

Right: The child of a tenant farmer stood in the doorway of her home in Greene County, Georgia, for this photograph taken in June 1941. *Jack Delano.*

This unidentified woman posed for a studio portrait in the 1930s.

Can the sister toting a briefcase stand with the sister on welfare? Can the sister behind a desk stand with the sister pushing a mop and bucket? Can the sister who wears her hair in dreadlocks stand with the sister who has a blond perm? Can the church sister stand with the sister from the mosque? I believe we can and we must.

—Mary A. Mitchell, *Chicago Sun-Times,* October 9, 1997

IT WOULD PROBABLY BE impossible to overestimate the importance education has had for Black women. African Americans generally have seen in eduction a way out of their oppression, but for women, vulnerable as they have been to sexual harassment and abuse from employers, education has held a special place. It has been the path toward the protection this society offers to "the lady."

In the earliest years of slavery, in colonial America, slaveholders sometimes educated their servants so that they could read the Bible and hymnals and become better Christians. In 1704, for example, a white New Yorker founded the Catechism School for slaves at Trinity Church. In 1793, a Black woman named Catherine Ferguson opened an integrated Sunday school in her home, offering religious instruction and life skills. Her church learned of this school and gave it a home as well as instructors who could teach the literacy skills that Ferguson could not. In the early 1830s, Sarah Mapps Douglass—who came from a well-to-do Black family and had been educated at home—opened a high school for Black girls in Philadelphia, the first of its kind in the country.

In the antebellum years in the South, however, the slaveholding class feared that educated slaves would rebel. The states passed laws against teaching Black Americans to read, and individual slave owners severely punished any enslaved person caught with reading material. Nonetheless, in 1819, a Black woman from Santo Domingo named Julian Froumountaine opened a free school for African Americans in Savannah, Georgia, one of many in the South. When restrictive laws were passed in the 1830s, Froumountaine went underground, teaching secretly for the rest of the decade. Elizabeth Lange opened a school for French-speaking Black immigrants from the Caribbean, where she had been born, and eventually founded an order of Black nuns dedicated to education, the Oblate Sisters of Providence. Another Black woman, Catherine Deveaux, started an underground school in 1838 and taught in secret for twenty-five years. Milla Granson, an enslaved woman, managed to persuade her master's children in Kentucky to teach her to read. When she was sold down the river to Mississippi, she secretly taught classes at night on her new plantation.

After slavery, education became a mission. Northern Black women streamed into the South to teach the newly freed. "In a single generation," wrote W. E. B. DuBois, "[Black women] put thirty thousand Black teachers in the South; they wiped out the illiteracy of the majority of the Black people of the land." Black women continued to fulfill this sacred duty through the Jim Crow years. The teacher in a Black community, especially in the rural South, often served as nurse, accountant, social worker, and counselor as well. She shaped not only minds but characters.

Black women also led the move for equal educational opportunity for their students. Ironically, when integration combined schools and thereby reduced faculties, Black women teachers were fired in disproportionate numbers. But when the failure of the contemporary educational system in our country became apparent, Black women were in the forefront of those who presented alternatives. Education is today, as it has been for almost four centuries, a primary value in the lives of Black women in America.

Overleaf: Anna Julia Cooper, principal of the famous M Street High School in Washington, D.C., was the fourth African American woman to earn a Ph.D. Studying only during her summers off from teaching, she attended Columbia University and then the Sorbonne in Paris, receiving her doctorate in 1925 when she was 66 years old.

In colonial schools, such as this one in Rhode Island, Black and Native American children were often taught together by missionaries, including Black women.

Below: In 1833, the citizens of Canterbury, Connecticut, tried ostracizing, fines, manure in the well, and finally fire to shut down a school for Black girls. The caption of this engraving from the *American Anti-Slavery Almanac* of 1839 read: "When schools have been established for colored scholars, the law-makers and the mob have combined to destroy them;—as at Canterbury, Conn., at Canaan, N.H., Aug. 10, 1835, at Zanesville and Brown Co., Ohio, in 1836."

These girls in the Colored Orphan Asylum received their education at the institution. This picture was taken on Good Friday, 1861. On July 11, 1863, the building was burned to the ground by draft rioters. The children were evacuated safely. © *Collection of the New-York Historical Society.*

This detail from a rare photograph by Jacob Riis, entitled *The First Board of Election Inspectors in the Beach Street Industrial School,* shows an African American girl in the student government of a school in New York City in the 1890s.

There are no people that need all the benefits resulting from a well-directed education more than we do. The condition of our people, the wants of our children, and the welfare of our race demand the aid of every helping hand. It is a work of time, a labor of patience, to become an effective school teacher; and it should be a work of love in which they who engage should not abate heart or hope until it is done.

—Frances E. W. Harper, 1852

This photograph, taken in 1890, shows a mother and daughter reading together in Mt. Meigs, Alabama. It was a common scene in the decades following the Civil War, as old taught young and young taught old. *Rudolf Eickemeyer.*

An unnamed Black teacher appears in this photograph with two of her white students in the plains of northern Wyoming in the 1890s.

Below: This group of girls, with their teacher, had their photograph taken at a school in Guthrie, Oklahoma, at the turn of the century.

Now, on graduation day, Papa said to me, "Daughter, you are college material. You owe it to your nation, your race, and yourself to go. And if you don't, then shame on you!" Well, it seemed to me that I had no choice but to go on with my schooling.

—Sarah Delany, *Having Our Say: The Delany Sisters' First 100 Years,* by Sarah L. Delany and A. Elizabeth Delany (with Amy Hill Hearth)

Above: Students at Tuskegee Institute wove hats and cane backs for chairs as part of the school's focus on vocational training. *C. M. Battey.*

Top left: Spelman students in the 1890s were of all ages, as Black women strove to catch up educationally. One of the women seen here is even pregnant.

Bottom left: Women students posed on the steps of Miner Hall at Howard University in 1893.

Three students went by boat to Penn School on St. Helena Island,
South Carolina, from nearby Palawana Island in about 1906.
Leigh Richmond Miner.

A WPA teacher instructed her literacy students in Birmingham, Alabama, in 1938. The woman in white is Julia Wilson, 87, who had just learned to read and write.

While it's great to be Black and beautiful . . . it's even better to be Black and beautiful and prepared.

—Martina Arroyo

A home economics class at the Bethune-Cookman Institute in Daytona Beach, Florida, worked under the inspiring words of Mary McLeod Bethune in February 1943. *Gordon Parks.*

Right: Students in a cooking class displayed the biscuits they had just baked at the Penn School in 1942.

Above: Children at the U.S. Housing Project, Ohio 5-2, took an art class from a WPA teacher in June 1940.

An unidentified schoolgirl waited for a bus in a small town in Tennessee in September 1943. *Esther Bubley.*

This picture of Marietta Sisnette in cap and gown, proudly holding her diploma, was taken upon her graduation from high school in 1938.

A plantation worker with no place to leave her child brought him to a WPA literacy class in Lafayette Parish, Louisiana, about 1940.

In 1946, the NAACP published a pamphlet focusing on the inequities of segregated education.

Below: The original photograph taken for the pamphlet.

Elsie Neely was teaching the sixth grade at the time of this photograph. She is shown here playing basketball with students Kim Hatcher and Arlene Burroughs. *Ken Heinen.*

I'm teaching students lessons of respect. I want these kids to learn more than just the ABC's. I want them to take pride in the Richfield Police Department, to have respect for the school nurse. I want to teach life skills and survival skills. . . . Give me the downtrodden kids, the kids at risk, the kids just sitting around watching TV. And when I hear that child shout, "I got it!" and see them flourish, I'm just tickled brown.

—Nel Johnson, Alabama schoolteacher, *Minneapolis Star Tribune,* June 22, 1997

BUILDING AND MAINTAINING a community has never been a luxury for African Americans. In order to survive, physically and spiritually, Black women and men have had to work together and offer each other shelter from the depredations of white America. The earliest communities included both Black captives and white indentured workers, who occupied a similar position. However, as slavery was refined legally and in custom, a virtually uncrossable divide opened between the races, and the Black community began to develop the characteristics that helped its members survive for the next three centuries.

In slave communities, on plantations and large farms, a separate ethic developed for dealings with the slaveholder and his minions. In that ethic, deceit was wholly acceptable. Back in the slave quarters, however, honesty was valued as strongly as in any other society. Most Black women taught their children to help the weakest do their work, to protect each other from the slaveholder, never to help the slaveholder against another slave, and to respect the authority of the elders in the community. All these values helped the community and its members to survive.

Another source of strength was religion. At first, enslaved people practiced the religions they brought with them from Africa. Later, most converted to Christianity, although many of their African beliefs and practices were incorporated into this new religion. By the beginning of the nineteenth century, the Black church had come into being, and women were its foundation.

Women have always been greatly in the majority in the Black church, and although they have only recently been accepted into leadership roles, they have made music, given testimony, offered prayers, and raised funds. And the church has given them sustenance. There were also a few women, even in the nineteenth century, who believed that they were called by God to preach, and that His authority was greater than that of their religious brethren. Jarena Lee, Zilpha Elaw, Rebecca Cox Jackson, and others went out from the established church and preached to whoever would listen to them.

Alongside the church were the various organizations that Black women created to serve the community. Early on, there were mutual benefit societies, created to provide the rudiments of social services. By 1838 there were 119 Black mutual aid societies in Philadelphia alone, more than half of which were female associations. Women made up nearly two-thirds of the membership of all Black benefit societies. Later in the nineteenth century, women's clubs began to take over the tradition of service, as did Black sororities still later.

That tradition provided the spirit and the skills for open resistance in the twentieth century. Community women were at the forefront of the fight for civil rights. By the late twentieth century, they were also taking their rightful position in the leadership of the church. Today, it is no longer possible to make a distinction between women's "clubs" and activist groups. The leaders of the nineteenth-century women's club movement would doubtless feel right at home in the National Coalition of 100 Black Women, a networking group for Black professional women.

Overleaf: This detail of a larger 1863 photograph (see page 167) shows women who are probably contrabands (escaped slaves) working at the Freedmen's Hospital in Nashville, Tennessee.

The respect that the slaves had for their owners might have been from fear, but the real character of a slave was brought out by the respect that they had for each other. Most of the time there was no force back of the respect the slaves had for each other, and yet, they were for the most part truthful, loving and respectful to one another.

—Jane Pyatt, Federal Writers Project interview

The entire enslaved community of J. J. Smith's plantation near Beaufort, South Carolina, gathered to be photographed by Union photographer T. H. O'Sullivan in 1862.

These slave quarters at the Perseverance plantation in Goose Creek Parish, South Carolina, were photographed for a *carte-de-visite* between 1860 and 1863. © *Collection of the New-York Historical Society.*

Right: This building functioned as the Freedmen's Hospital in Nashville, Tennessee, in July 1863.

Mis' Bessie fixed me up to be baptized at the Limestone Baptist Church. We had to go to the spring pond called Austin's Pond, where all the baptizing took place. . . . When we got there, the banks of Austin's Pond was lined with Negroes shouting and singing glory and praises. . . . When my time come, I started to the pond, and just before the preacher turned to take my hand, I shouted, "Lord, have mercy," and clapped my hands over my head. Somebody said, "That child sure is getting a new soul."

—Easter Lockhart, Federal Writers Project interview

Observers both Black and white were accepted at this 1896 baptism in Virginia. *Huestis Cook.*

Right: This photograph is captioned "Mother Brown and Child Ruth/Rescued from Port Tampa City Midnight Saturday "Jan" 23rd "09./ Picture made by Travelers tree. W. P. Beach. March 3rd "09./ Tree used to supply water to thirsty travelers through the desert. Will you help me to pray for this child./ Yours in love, Mother Brown."

Bottom right: The caption to this photograph from the 1880s identifies its subject as "Rev. Mrs. J. H. Vigal of Buffalo, N.Y." Since no major denominations ordained women until much later, she may have been an itinerant preacher, like Jarena Lee.

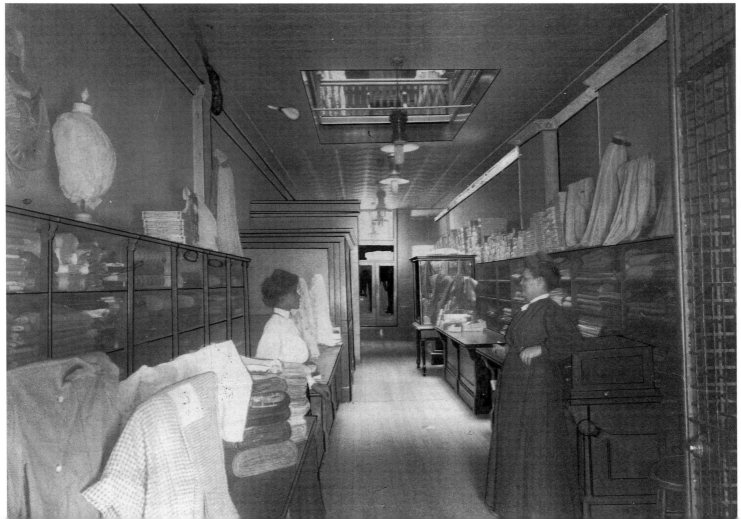

Top left: When Maggie Lena Walker took over the Order of St. Luke, a mutual benefit society, in 1899, she reorganized it according to the philosophy that the Black community should be economically independent of the white community. She converted the funeral benefits into an insurance company in 1900, published a newspaper in 1902, and founded a bank in 1903. The St. Luke Penny Savings Bank separated from the rest of the order to comply with banking and insurance regulations. It combined with other Black banks to form the Consolidated Bank and Trust Company, with Maggie Walker as chairman of the board. It still prospers today.

Bottom left: The Order of St. Luke opened a department store that served the Black community in 1905. Maggie Lena Walker also believed in providing both employment and leadership positions for women. Shown here are the manager of the Emporium, Rosa E. Watson, and the dry goods manager, Sallie M. Bullock.

Nannie Helen Burroughs and the Women's Convention, an auxiliary of the National Baptist Convention (or Black Baptist Church), founded the National Training School for Women in 1909. These NTSW students were probably photographed in the late 1920s or early 1930s.

Above: This beautiful portrait of Penn School students Mabel Grant and Eveline Black was taken about 1906. *Leigh Richmond Miner.*

Top left: Unusually informal for 1897, this shot by photographer Henry Arthur Taft is thought to be of two staff members of Agassiz Hall, Martha's Vineyard Summer Institute, where Taft was staying in connection with an amateur photography club.

Bottom left: These formerly enslaved women were attending a convention in Washington, D.C., in 1916 when this photograph was taken.

Left: Before becoming a member of the Baha'i religion, Dorothy Champ was a star on Broadway. She was one of many who felt that Baha'i's multiculturalism would help bring the races together.

Right: Diane Fletcher, who lived with the Kiowa people, posed for this portrait wearing moccasins, a piano shawl for a skirt, a bell pull for a belt, and a Chinese-style shirt.

A Mormon couple posed in Utah around the turn of the century.

These Cape Verdean immigrants were photographed for an article in the New Bedford *Standard Times.* Aboard the ship *Savoia,* they arrived in New Bedford on October 4, 1914.

Above: These women obviously turned many heads as they enjoyed a Sunday stroll on 7th Avenue in 1938. *Austin Hansen.*

Top right: These women were canning greens in preparation for sale in southeastern Missouri in May 1938. *Russell Lee.*

Bottom right: Possibly taking a break from their Saturday shopping, these new mothers exchanged the news in Greensboro, Georgia, in 1941. *Jack Delano.*

Above: These migrant workers were photographed in 1941 outside the Pahokee "hotel," where they lived. *Marion Post Wolcott.*

Left: This 1936 WPA photograph shows mattress makers in Savannah, Georgia, having dinner together in the open air.

You was named a so-and-so first; whose child you was came after that. If you was bad they'd spank you and then tell your people. Any of your people they'd find. And it was like they'd told your mama, dad, or grandparents. Anyone would be on you 'cause you'd been a shame to the family—not just the peoples raising you up or just your mama and dad. Everybody in Rainbow Springs had it just the same.

—"Ora Fisher," quoted by Elizabeth Clark-Lewis in *Living in, Living Out*

This 1939 photograph, entitled *Harlem Street Scene,* shows the vibrant, communal aspect of city life during the Depression. *Sid Grossman.*

I can't think of anyone who wasn't trying to be half-decent. That's going to church sometime, anyway. I know many a man come up from Success [Virginia] and just stand around the church—not go in once to a year— but was steady coming up to church anyhow. If you was young you had to come—because somebody wanted you to come. When you courted you came because you wanted somebody. After that, you'd just come to be a somebody to people down there in Rixeyville. And what you got there stayed with you, for sure, every day of your life. I know in my life it's a fact.

—"Marie Stone," quoted by Elizabeth Clark-Lewis in *Living in, Living Out*

The churchyard was a favorite gathering place on Sunday morning, even for those who were not particularly religious. This 1941 photograph shows men and women outside their church in Harmony Community, Georgia. *Irving Rusinow.*

Left: The Great Migration transported thousands of Black Southerners who were accustomed to their own small churches. Many of them recreated their idea of church in urban storefronts. In 1943, Godfrey Frankel took this photograph, entitled *After Church,* of the Holy Church of Christ, which was located in an alley in southwest Washington, D.C.

Below: Many African Americans in urban areas have been devout Catholics, such as these women attending a service at St. Elizabeth's on Chicago's South Side in 1942. *Jack Delano.*

Right: This photograph, entitled *Nation Sisters,* shows Black Muslim women at a Savior's Day gathering at the Chicago Coliseum in 1966. *Robert Sengestacke.*

Street life was active in 1960s Chicago, despite urban blight. *James Stricklin.*

This is the Berlin Wall right over here. You see, you don't even have a ten-cent store. Woolworth doesn't find it profitable. We don't have a bank. . . . So if you want to get your check cashed, I go downtown to the bank. I usually go to Sears or Wards or somewhere where I've got a charge account. This is where you get a check cashed, unless you want to go to the currency exchange and pay somebody to get your check cashed. . . . We don't have any facilities here that poor folks need. On Michigan Avenue, where people can get along without it, you got your ten-cent stores.

—Lucy Jefferson, interview with Studs Terkel for *Division Street, America*

Self Portrait with Auntie Lily, from the series "Nappy Heads," Ansonia, Connecticut, 1997. *Lydia Ann Douglas.*

Million Woman Mom. The Million Woman March of 1997 brought together between 500,000 and 1,000,000 women in Philadelphia, including this mother. *Salimah Ali. © Salimah Ali, 1997.*

Everywhere I turned I saw beautiful black women—all shapes, sizes, and colors. Just beautiful faces—different hairstyles, different clothing. Different everything but with one mission. That mission was to get together with sisters and find out what needed to be done to better ourselves and our community.

—Alisha Henry, Michigan State University pre-law student, 1997

THE SUN RISES OVER A HILL in the early morning. People are gathering from all directions, in pairs and small groups, sleepy but talking and laughing quietly. Some carry musical instruments—drums and hollow sticks, perhaps banjoes and fifes. Suddenly a rhythm starts up near the top of the hill, pounded out on a small drum. In a moment, the rhythm is picked up and augmented by the pat of feet on hard ground. A woman begins to dance, slowly and with exquisite grace. The crowd gathers around her, leaving a clearing for her dance. The time is the 1700s. The place is New England. The event is a slave festival, and it may go on for days, as enslaved men and women dance away the sorrows of their lives and rejoice in their families and friends.

In New Orleans every Sunday and on church holy days in Congo Square, dancing started at three o'clock in the afternoon and went on until nine o'clock at night. The drumming and chanting and dancing were performed by both men and women. Sometimes the dancers kept on until they dropped from exhaustion.

In almost every situation throughout their history, African American women have found a way to play, to relieve their sufferings and celebrate their joys in movement, music, and laughter. As children, they have skipped rope, climbed trees, run footraces, and strung berries for necklaces. As adults, they have attended concerts, gone to nightclubs, and run along beaches. Ultra-respectable college students of the nineteenth century took time out from their labors for the uplift of the race to have snowball fights and picnics. Field laborers gathered after sparse dinners to laugh and gossip at a quilting bee. Domestic workers squeezed their tired feet into dancing shoes for a night on the town.

There has been less play than work, most of the time. And sometimes there was no play at all. But usually Black women have proved as resourceful in creating opportunities for pleasure and recreation as in stretching the loaves and fishes of their lives to feed themselves and their families.

Black women participated in dances and slave festivals, not only as dancers, but also as instrumentalists and "juber rhymers." This depiction is by an unknown artist.

They gathered Marster's big corn crop and arranged it in long, high piles, and sometimes it took several days for them corn shuckers to get it all shucked, but everybody stayed right on the job til it was finished. At night, they worked by the light of big fires and torches. Then, they had the big supper and started dancing. They stopped so often to swig that corn liquor Marster provided for them, that before midnight folks started falling out and dropping down in the middle of the dance ring. The others would get them by the heels and drag them off to one side, til they come to and was ready to drink more liquor and dance again.

—Cordelia Thomas, Federal Writers Project interview

One of the slaves, my aunt, she was a royal slave. She could dance all over the place with a tumbler of water on her head, without spilling it. She sure could tote herself. I always loved to see her come to church. She sure could tote herself.

—Hannah Crasson, Federal Writers Project interview

This watercolor painting was made in Lynchburg, Virginia, in 1853, by artist Lewis Miller.

I was escorted to a concert last night by Senator Bruce of Miss. The single ladies here rave over his good looks—he is goodlooking or rather very fine looking but I do not especially admire him. He is a great big good natured lump of fat. He wears the finest broadcloth, a lovely beaver, the finest linen, diamond studs and his wellshaped hands are encased in the loveliest kids. He is gentlemanly and very jolly. Just the fellow to go around with. It is customary for Senator Bruce, Representative Lynch and myself to attend evening church, concerts &c in company. The beautiful ladies are quite disgusted and say in the hearing of the gentlemen "There goes that heartless Emma Brown, with no style and no beauty. What Bruce sees in her, or Lynch either is difficult to imagine." The gentlemen are exceedingly amused at these comments and appear more devoted.

—From a letter by Emma Brown to Emily Howland, March 31, 1875.
Miss Brown was a teacher in Washington, D.C.

In theaters in most cities in the 19th century, African Americans were able to buy tickets only for the *Negro gallery*, as this engraving is entitled. Date and source unknown.

Elizabeth Taylor Greenfield, the first African American musician to earn a reputation in both the United States and Britain, was born into slavery but sang in a command performance before Queen Victoria. This engraving of "The Black Swan" appeared in P. T. Barnum's short-lived magazine *The Illustrated News,* April 2, 1853. © *Collection of the New-York Historical Society.*

Below: The first annual ball of the Skidmore Guard, a black military organization, was held at the Seventh Avenue Germania Assembly Rooms in 1872. This engraving was published in *Frank Leslie's Illustrated Newspaper* on February 24, 1872.

A different class frequented the "Black and Tan," a dive on Thompson Street on the Lower East Side of New York in the 1880s. Thompson Street was called "the borderland where the black and white races meet in common debauch." *Richard Hoe Lawrence.* © *Collection of the New-York Historical Society.*

These fashionable ladies were photographed by Frances Benjamin Johnson at the 1903 Minnesota State Fair in St. Paul.

Contestants in a Texas beauty pageant rode in a parade down the main street of Bonham, Texas, in 1910.

Below: Sometime around 1900, Truth and Grace Hannah posed with their catch after a successful fishing trip on their family's Nebraska homestead. The Hannahs were among more than fifty thousand Black Americans who moved west to escape Jim Crow toward the end of the 19th century.

These two girls were photographed in a mining camp.

Swimming!!

Clowning around for the camera, two unidentified women posed in a mock automobile in the 1910s.

Below: Langston Hughes snapped this shot of Zora Neale Hurston in the 1920s.

Foreshadowing Tiger Woods, this young girl showed good form with a
stick and a rock for a Detroit Publishing Company photographer in 1905.

There is an inscription on the back of this snapshot, taken in Oklahoma or Texas in the 1910s, that says, "For Pete's sake don't show this one to the fellows, for I wouldn't have one of them get it for the world."

Right: This whimsical photograph carries only the inscription "Thanksgiving 1912."

Below: These teachers from the Penn School in South Carolina took time out from their labors to have a picnic and a run on the beach in 1921.

Alma mater of Ida B. Wells, Rust College was founded in 1866 by the Methodist Church as a coeducational Black school. This picture of the women's basketball team was taken in the early twentieth century.

Howard University coeds turned out in fashionable attire for
a big game in the 1920s. *Addison Scurlock.*

This photograph of children playing ball in the schoolyard was taken at Booker T. Washington School in Louisville, Kentucky, in the early 1940s for the Public Health Service, probably by Marion Post Wolcott.

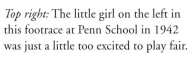

Top right: The little girl on the left in this footrace at Penn School in 1942 was just a little too excited to play fair.

Big car, little girl. Oklahoma, 1941.

I walk down the street, I smoke a cigarette. Well, ladies aren't supposed to do that. But I'm no lady. [Laughs] I just have the best old time. Sometimes, it amuses, you know. When I get blue and disgusted, I go get me some beer and get cockeyed drunk, stay at home. I don't go out. I don't believe in taverns. Then you say, why the hell do you drink beer? Because I like it.

—Lucy Jefferson, interview with Studs Terkel for *Division Street, America*

Two women visited over a potluck dinner at a ministers' meeting in Yanceyville, North Carolina, in October 1940. *Marion Post Wolcott.*

Right: Cheers.

William and Mildred Shaw enjoyed a night out on the town with Grant and Mattie Jackson and an unknown woman in the early 1940s.

Right: People were not always depressed during the Depression. This couple clearly had a great time on a night out in Clarksdale, Mississippi, in 1939 in this detail from a photo by Marion Post Wolcott.

I think it was the first weekend we were there that she [Vi Burnside] came down to our club, the Ebony Lounge. And the place was packed. Now, I had a brand-new instrument, all pretty and shiny. So Vi asked if she could borrow my horn. I said sure. And she got up there and turned the place out. She played every note that was supposed to be in everything! So I knew that was it. The next week I went over to see her at her club, a place called Gleason's. When the people saw me, they demanded that I play, so she gave me her horn. And when I left there they put so much money in the bell of that saxophone! I'll never forget it. I had a bell full of money and a chicken dinner!

—Willene Barton, quoted by Linda Dahl in *Stormy Weather:
The Music and Lives of a Century of Jazz Women* (1984).

The 1950s were a time when America believed its own press.
These Girl Scouts enjoyed some wholesome, all-American fun
while pretending to have a cookout. *Robert H. McNeill.*

I had four children, and they were in the 4-H and the Boy Scouts. They could go to the swimming pool, but they had to sit on the side while the other [white] children would do the swimming. We went to the drug store, and you know, back in those days children licked their ice cream cones. If you were black, you'd have to go outside to lick your cone. If you wanted to go to the show, and if you knew the black man that worked for the Pruitts, you could sit on the stairs and look at the show, but you couldn't go and sit in the seats. So three of us got together, and I said, "We're going to have to make a change in this because I do not want to pay fifteen cents"—and that's a little thing now—"to take my children on the bus to Indianapolis and walk all the way out to the Walker Theater for them to go and see these little cowboy shows and things like that."

We went down to the drugstore first and ordered some dishes of ice cream. The man brought it to us, and we went to sit down at the table. He said, "Well, you know I'm sorry Cassie, but you can't eat that in here." And I said, "Oh?" And he said, "No." And I said, "I just want to know why?" He said, "Well, you know I depend on transit trade, and some of the people might be coming through here and see you colored people sitting here, and they may not want to eat. I might lose business." So we just sat that ice cream right back in the saucer, just like it was, and went right on out. Then we went over to the show and just marched right on in. The lady started shaking her head the first thing. I just let her shake her head. We went right in there. She didn't want to sell us a ticket. But we just went on, laid the money down, went on in, and sat down. Well, you know, after that there wasn't a thing said anymore, and we continued to go to the show from that night and are still going.

—Cassie Swarm, Black Women in the Middle West Project

Wilma Rudolph became an American hero when she won three gold medals at the 1960 Olympic Games. She was honored throughout the United States and toured to fifteen countries as a goodwill ambassador. Awards piled up and fans mobbed airports. But there was another side to the lives of Black women who competed in the Olympics. Rudolph and her family still lived in a government housing project.

Mae [Faggs] would always tell me, "If you can keep up with me, you are doing fine." So she said to me, "As long as you can keep up with me you are doing fine and remember this is the last race."

So I said, "okay," and went back to my blocks. I think she was in the third lane and I was in the fifth or sixth. I wasn't close to her and I was used to running close to her in practice, so I was nervous about that. So I did remember the gun going off and I looked up to find her and she was a long way in front of me, so I said to myself, "I am going to try to catch her," and I caught her and we had the same time. Afterward she teased me and said, "Skeeter, I told you to keep up with me, I didn't tell you to pass me."

—Wilma Rudolph describing how she earned a place on the 1956 U.S. Olympic team at the age of 15

Olympic medal winner Earlene Brown almost didn't make it to the Tokyo Olympics. For some reason, the AAU in 1960 required athletes to pay for their own passports. To get one, Brown borrowed a friend's car and withdrew her last $4.30 from her checking account. She put $2 worth of gas in the car, paid $2 for passport photos, and used two of her last dimes on phone calls trying to borrow money for the passport fee. Finally, a journalist lent her the money. *Lartz.*

Below: The legendary Althea Gibson was the first Black woman to play in the top ranks of professional tennis. She also played on the Ladies' Professional Golf Association tour for seven years and was author of the autobiography *I Always Wanted to Be Somebody.*

The three women pictured here—Mrs. Waltyes Doyles, Mrs. Elizabeth Jenkins, and Mrs. Ruth Lieghston—were members of the Baltimore chapter of the Northeasterners Club. A group for Black professional women formed in 1948, the Club ultimately had 13 chapters nationally. This photograph was probably taken sometime between 1958 and 1960 when the women took a break from a Northeasterners convention to go for a short cruise on the yacht *Fla-Joe,* owned by Dr. Joseph Henry Thomas of Turner's Station, Maryland.

Right: This family enjoyed the boats for hire at Jones Lake, a Black park in North Carolina. The photograph's original caption reads, in part, "Over 1000 Negroes use the bath-house each week, and many more use other facilities on which there is no count. This growing use, and the fact that the patrons have taken exceeding good care of their park, has convinced officials that other parks should be set up in the state."

Photographer Irving Georges snapped this photograph of his friends at play, sometime in 1974 or 1975, at 147th Street and 8th Avenue.

A dancer captured the crowd's attention at an African street
festival in Harlem in 1984. *Lydia Ann Douglas.*

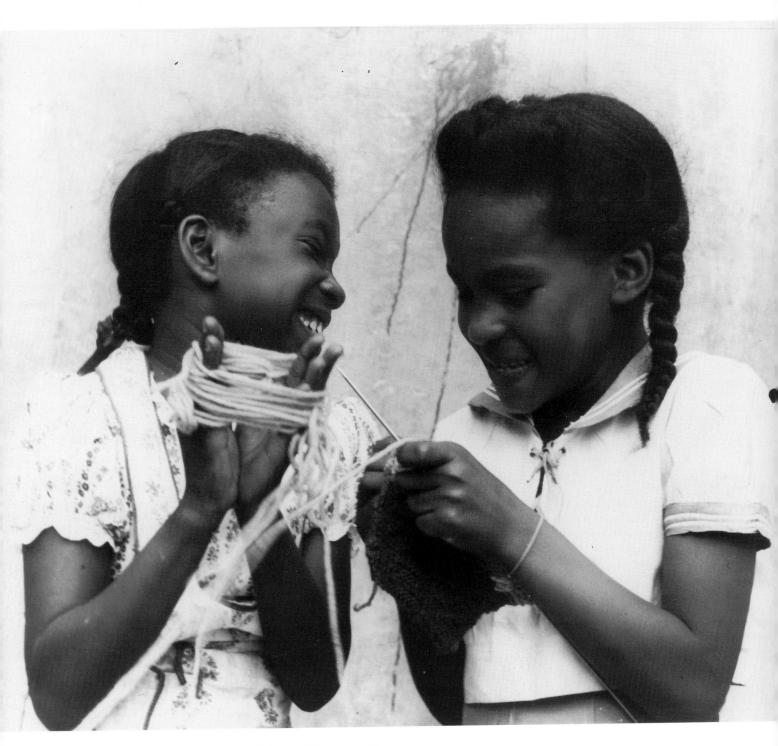

Photographer Florence Ward captured the joy of these two girls on a
Harlem playground. *Florence Ward.*

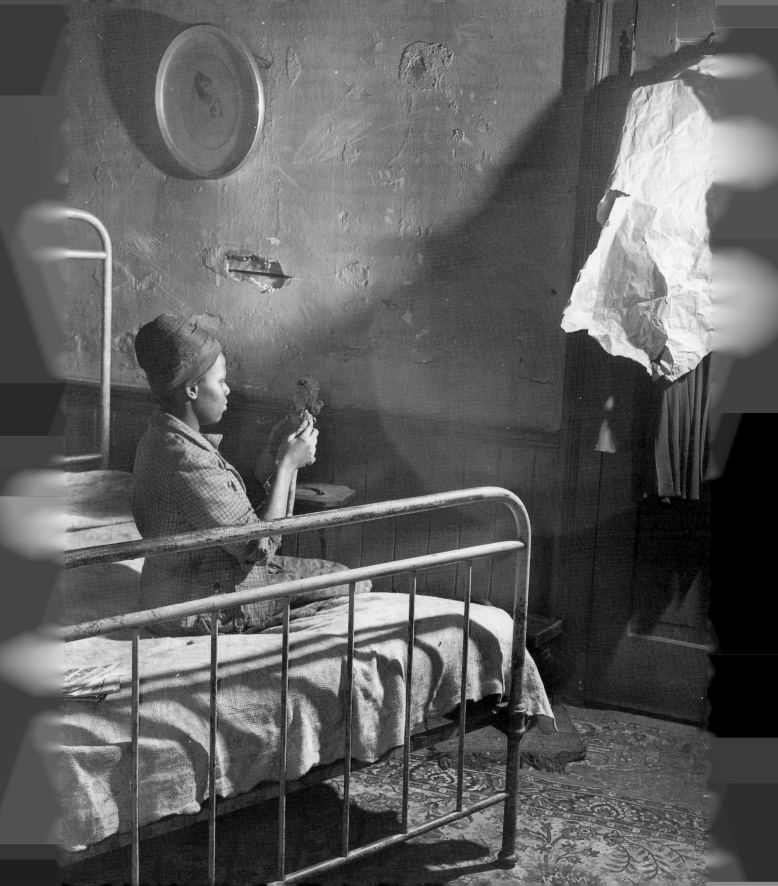

BLACK WOMEN HAVE VALUED HIGHLY their families and their communities. They have put their faith in education and worked enormously hard to disseminate its benefits. But these values alone do not explain the strength of African American women. For that, we need to look inside. Throughout their history, Black women have cultivated an inner strength that has enabled them to withstand hatred and scorn, to face down their oppressors, and even to enjoy their lives. In part, that strength comes from religious beliefs. In part, it is drawn from other Black women. And in part, it comes from shielding their personal truths from those who oppress them.

An enslaved woman often hid herself in secrecy and silence from slaveholders. She could not win most of the daily battles she faced, so she created a space inside that was the home of her true self. If she was forced to bow and scrape to white masters, there was a woman inside whose head remained always raised. If she had to accept an insult to her dignity, the woman inside was untouched. Black women shared these secret selves only with other Black women. Even Black men, as potential oppressors themselves, were not often privy to this inner personhood.

After emancipation, Black women continued to cultivate the inner strength that could help them survive. Their spiritual sustenance included the quilts they made, the songs they sang, the poems they wrote. From the love of their children and their God, they drew nourishment. In kitchens and beauty shops, their stories and laughter and sweetness fed each other.

In recent years, Black women have begun to break some of the silences that have protected them for so long. They have taken this risk because it is necessary, for themselves and for their daughters. It is also necessary to maintain, nonetheless, the inner space that has allowed Black women to remain psychically whole and spiritually sound.

> You must sit quietly without a chip [on your shoulder]. Not sodden—and weighted as if your feet were cast in the iron of your soul. Not wasting strength in enervating gestures as if two hundred years of bonds and whips had really tricked you into nervous uncertainty.
>
> But quiet; quiet. Like Buddha who—brown like I am—sat entirely at ease, entirely sure of himself; motionless and knowing, a thousand years before the white man knew there was so very much difference between feet and hands.
>
> Motionless on the outside. But inside?
>
> Silent.
>
> Still . . . "Perhaps Buddha is a woman."
>
> So you too. Still; quiet; with a smile, ever so slight, at the eyes so that Life will flow into and not by you. And you can gather, as it passes, the essences, the overtones, the tints, the shadows; draw understanding to your self.
>
> And then you can, when Time is ripe, swoop to your feet—at your full height—at a single gesture.
>
> Ready to go where?
>
> Why . . . Wherever God motions.

Unidentified woman, South Carolina or Louisiana, 1929–1931. *Doris Ulmann.*

Unidentified woman, 1903. The original caption read, "Her Day's Work Is Done."
E. J. Davison.

*Mostly the way I dealt with racial prejudice is that I have a deep feeling of my own
worth, and nobody can take that away from me. White people aren't that important to me.
Difficult Black people aren't important to me. I don't think you have to go through life
miserable to make somebody else happy. And I never have.*

—Elizabeth Bridgwaters, Black Women in the Middle West Project

Right: Miss Celia Simmons, a midwife on St. Helena Island, South Carolina, 1906.
Leigh Richmond Miner.

She knew things that nobody had ever told her. For instance, the words of the trees and the wind. She often spoke to falling seeds and said, "Ah hope you fall on soft ground," because she had heard seeds saying that to each other as they passed.

—Zora Neale Hurston, *Their Eyes Were Watching God*

Every time I put on uniforms I knew in myself it wouldn't be for always.

—"Pernella Ross," quoted by Elizabeth Clark-Lewis in
Living In, Living Out

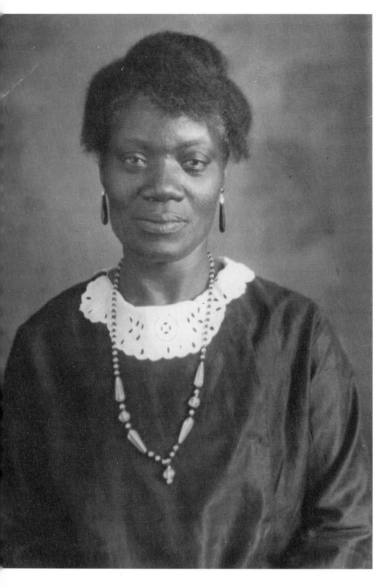

Unidentified woman, South Carolina, 1920s. This woman insisted on having her portrait made both in and out of her maid's uniform. *Richard Samuel Roberts.*

Facing page: Unidentified woman, Orange County, North Carolina, September 1939. The original caption read, "Dipping snuff while watching farmers making sorghum syrup." *Marion Post Wolcott.*

Aunt Mary, 1928. *Addison Scurlock.*

It is the inner life that develops the outer, and if we are in earnest the precious things lie all around our feet.

—Frances E. W. Harper, centennial of the Pennsylvania Society for the Abolition of Slavery in 1875

Unidentified woman, Greene County, Georgia, June 1941.
Jack Delano.

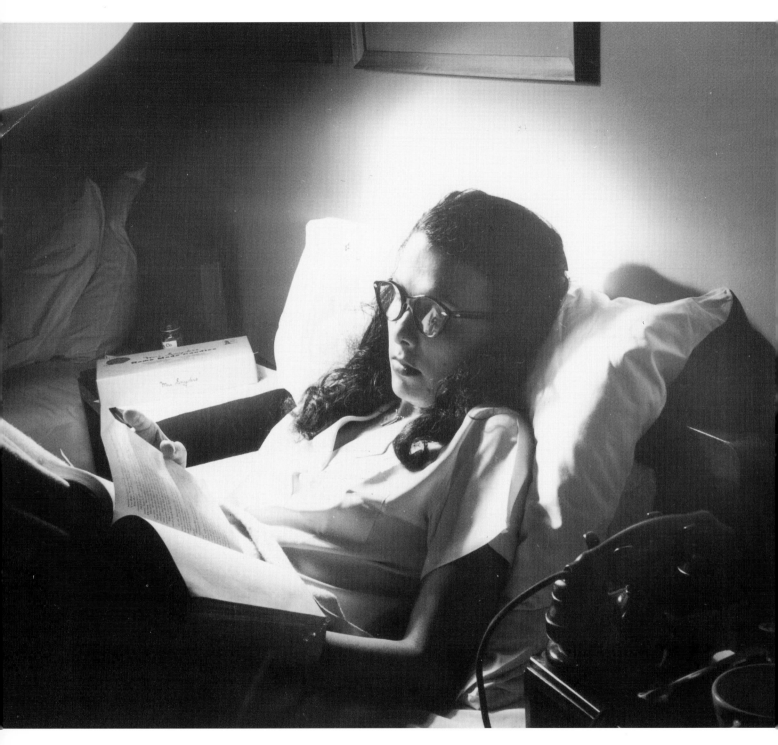

Lena Horne, Chicago, 1950.

Activist Modjeska Simkins, South Carolina, ca. late 1970s.

234

Orange-picker's daughter, Daytona Beach, Florida,
February 1943. *Gordon Parks.*

Left: A St. Helena woman, possibly named Bessie
Middleton, 1942 or 1943.

I am sure there is pain waiting in my life. The whole world situation is painful. But I am here to tell you that your joy can equal your pain—it can strip your pain. And if you can have faith in a God that somebody else gave you and that you have never seen, you can also have faith in your own joy—something you've at least had a glimmer of.

—Alice Walker, *Essence,* July 1992

Unidentified migrant worker, Belcross, North Carolina, July 1940. *Jack Delano.*

Left: Unidentified woman, ca. 1890s. The original caption read, "Young woman in men's clothing."

Luceal Allen, 17th Street Market, Richmond, Virginia, December 1980. *Amir M. Pishdad.*

We cannot direct the wind, but we can adjust the sails.

—Bertha Calloway

Sensuality, a portrait of Nathalie Richardson, New Haven, Connecticut, 1993. *Lydia Ann Douglas.*